# GMAT
## Direct

# GMAT

## Direct

### Streamlined Review and Strategic Practice from the Leader in GMAT Prep

PUBLISHING

New York

© 2009 Kaplan, Inc.

Published by Kaplan Publishing, a division of Kaplan, Inc.
1 Liberty Plaza, 24th Floor
New York, NY 10006

Printed in the United States of America

10  9  8  7  6  5  4  3  2  1

ISBN: 978-1-60714-250-8

Kaplan Publishing books are available at special quantity discounts to use for sales promotions, employee premiums, or educational purposes. Please email our Special Sales Department to order or for more information at *kaplanpublishing@kaplan.com,* or write to Kaplan Publishing, 1 Liberty Plaza, 24th Floor, New York, NY 10006.

# TABLE OF CONTENTS

## PART III: GMAT RESOURCES

## kaptest.com/publishing

The material in this book is up-to-date at the time of publication. However, the Graduate Admission Management Council may have instituted changes in the tests or test registration process after this book was published. Be sure to read carefully the materials you receive when you register for the test.

If there are any important late-breaking developments—or changes or corrections to the Kaplan test preparation materials in this book—we will post that information online at **kaptest.com/publishing.** Check to see if there is any information posted there regarding this book.

## kaplansurveys.com/books

What did you think of this book? We'd love to hear your comments and suggestions. We invite you to fill out our online survey form at **kaplansurveys.com/books.**

Your feedback is extremely helpful as we continue to develop high-quality resources to meet your needs.

# Part One

# THE GMAT

# CHAPTER 1: INTRODUCTION TO THE GMAT

For many aspiring business students, the Graduate Management Admission Test (GMAT) may be viewed as an obstacle. The exam is a long, grueling experience that few look forward to undertaking.

We at Kaplan, however, view the GMAT not as an obstacle but as an opportunity for you—and a wonderful one at that. How is that? How can such a long and unpleasant exam be anything but an annoyance? Well, for starters, it won't remain unpleasant once we show you how to crack the questions in record time. Furthermore, if you follow our advice to engage in plenty of realistic proctored practice before your actual GMAT, it won't feel long either!

Okay, so it might not be *annoying*, but how does that make it *wonderful*? Glad you asked.

Your GMAT score makes up a large part of the admissions decision, and unlike your GPA, you *can* improve it *drastically* in a relatively short period of time. If you're not happy with your GPA, the GMAT can be that second chance in life that you've always wanted. Moreover, if you are lucky enough to have a great GPA, a stellar GMAT score will underscore that fact.

Besides, if you're one of the thousands of MBA candidates who have chosen to gain some professional, real-world experience before getting their MBA, your GPA is ancient history. The longer you are out of school, the less accurate of an indicator that GPA will be of your academic prowess to admissions officers. The GMAT will be their best look at you *right now*.

*Anyone* **can be trained to do significantly better on the GMAT.** Once you've seen the proven Kaplan strategies in this book, we're sure that you'll agree.

## THE FORMAT

Your GMAT Test Day experience will last roughly four hours. Here's how it breaks down:

| Section Type | Question Type(s) | Number of Questions | Timing |
|---|---|---|---|
| Analytical Writing Assessment (AWA) | Essay | 2 | 30 minutes per essay |
| Optional Break | — | — | 10 minutes |
| Quantitative Section | Problem Solving Data Sufficiency | 37 | 75 minutes |
| Optional Break | — | — | 10 minutes |
| Verbal Section | Sentence Correction Reading Comprehension Critical Reasoning | 41 | 75 minutes |

So-called "experimental" questions will also be scattered throughout the test. They will look just like the other multiple-choice questions but won't contribute to your score.

The upcoming chapters will examine each of the question types in greater detail. For now, note the following: you'll be answering roughly 78 multiple-choice questions in 2.5 hours. That's less than two minutes per question *before* factoring in the time needed to read the reading passages. You'll obviously need to move quickly, but you can't let yourself get careless.

Taking control of the GMAT means increasing the *speed* of your work without sacrificing *accuracy*—and this book focuses on just that!

# THE CAT

The GMAT is a computer-adaptive test (CAT). A CAT is designed to assess your abilities using fewer test questions than traditional paper-based tests. There are several things that make a CAT unique:

- **CATs are administered on a day of your choice.** CATs are taken at a special testing center at a time you schedule. You will sit at a private workstation, though there will be other test takers around you.

- **CATs adapt to your performance.** The multiple-choice questions on a CAT will adjust to your ability level, so no two test takers will receive the exact same test. The questions are weighted according to their difficulty and other statistical properties—not according to their position in the test.

- **CATs are scored on two criteria.** The scoring is based on the number of questions answered—correct or otherwise—and the difficulty (and other statistical characteristics) of each question.

The computer-adaptive format of the GMAT takes some getting used to. In fact, it's pretty unusual at first. Here's how it works.

There's a large pool of potential questions ranging from moderately easy to very difficult. To start, you're given a question of moderate difficulty. If you get it right, the computer will give you a harder question next. If you get it wrong, however, the computer will give you an easier question next. In other words, the computer scores each question and then uses that information—along with your previous responses and the requirements of the test design—to determine which question to present next. The process continues throughout, and the computer will zero in on an accurate assessment of your ability level.

If you keep getting questions right, the test will get harder and harder; if you slip up and make some mistakes, it will adjust and start giving you easier problems. However, if you begin to answer those easier problems correctly, the test will go back to the harder ones.

Ideally, you are given enough questions to ensure that scores are not based on luck. If you get one hard question right, you might just have been lucky, but if you get ten hard questions right, then luck has little to do with it. Therefore, the test is self-adjusting and self-correcting.

You will only see one question at a time, and your answer determines the question that you get next. For this reason, you will be unable to skip forward or backward: you must answer every question in the order presented to you, and you cannot go back once you've confirmed an answer.

Random guessing can significantly lower your scores, so if you can't answer a question, you should eliminate as many wrong choices as you can and make the best educated guess of what's left.

Another major consequence of the GMAT format is that hard questions are worth more than easy ones. It has to be this way, because the very purpose of this adaptive format is to find your scoring level—the level at which you would get roughly half of the questions presented to you correct.

Imagine two students—one who does ten basic questions, half of which she gets right and half of which she gets wrong, and one who does ten very hard questions, half of which she gets right and half of which she gets wrong. The same number of questions has been answered correctly in each case, but this does not reflect an equal ability on the part of the two students. In fact, the student who got five out of ten hard questions wrong could still get a very high score on the GMAT, but in order to get to these tough questions, she first had to get medium-difficulty questions right.

Every time you get the question right, the computer raises your score and gives you a slightly harder question. Every time you get a question wrong, the computer lowers your score and gives you a slightly easier question. Therefore, while sticking to the basic questions means an easier test, you cannot earn a top score without getting to the hard ones.

## NAVIGATING THE GMAT: COMPUTER BASICS

Let's preview the primary computer functions that you will use to move around on the GMAT. The screen below is typical for an adaptive test.

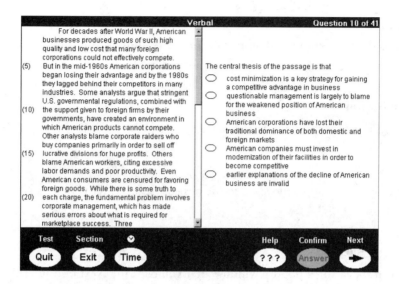

As you can see, there are empty bubbles for the answer choices—no letters (A), (B), (C), (D), (E). This is different from most multiple-choice tests.

To make the questions in this book appear as testlike as possible, the five answer choices in practice questions are not identified by letters. You will see blank ovals, just as you will on Test Day. However, for the purposes of discussion, we identify each answer choice using the corresponding letter in the answer explanation.

Here's what the various buttons do.

### The Time Button

Clicking on this button turns the time display at the top of the screen on and off. When you have five minutes left in a section, the clock flashes and the display changes from Hours/Minutes to Hours/Minutes/Seconds.

### The Exit Button

This allows you to exit the section before the time is up. If you budget your time wisely, you should never have to use this button—time will run out just as you are finishing the section.

### The Help Button

This one leads to directions and other stuff from the tutorial. You should know all this already, and besides, the test clock won't pause just because you click on Help.

### The Quit Button

Hitting this button ends the test.

### The Next Button

Hit this when you want to move on to the next question. After you press Next, you must hit Confirm.

### The Confirm Button

This button appears in a pop-up window after you click the Next button. The Confirm button tells the computer you are happy with your answer and are really ready to move to the next question. You cannot proceed until you have hit this button.

### The Scroll Bar

Similar to the scroll bar on a Windows-style computer display, the scroll bar is a thin, vertical column with up and down arrows at the top and bottom. Clicking on the arrows moves you up or down the page you're reading.

Now, let's have a look at the pros and cons of the CAT.

## ADVANTAGES OF THE CAT

The computer-adaptive format of the GMAT carries the following advantages over a traditional test:

### Convenience

The CAT is offered at hundreds of centers almost every day of the year. Registration can usually be done merely days in advance, though depending on the time of year and availability of testing centers in your area, you may need to register several weeks ahead for certain test dates.

### Length

Because the computer adjusts to your level, it won't need nearly as many questions as a traditional test would to gauge your ability accurately.

### Time

The CAT gives you more time to spend on each question than the paper-based test.

### Efficiency

Because the computer scores the multiple-choice portion as you work, you will receive your overall score immediately after the test, and your chosen schools will have it just 10–15 days later.

### Environment

There will only be a few other test takers in the room with you. It won't be like taking an exam in one of those massive lecture halls with distractions everywhere.

### Pacing

There's a timer at the top of the computer screen to help you pace yourself.

### Break

There's an optional pause after each section, and Kaplan recommends that you use it to stretch and relax.

## DISADVANTAGES OF THE CAT

The GMAT CAT also has the following disadvantages over a traditional test.

### Inflexibility

There is only one question on the screen at any time, and you must answer it before you get another. You cannot skip ahead, and you cannot go back to questions you've already answered.

### Distraction

If the person next to you is noisy or distracting, the proctor cannot move you or the other person because your test is on the computer.

### Confidence

Because the test will constantly present you with problems at your level, the vast majority of test takers, whether they're doing well or not, will feel like they are struggling through the test.

### Notes

You can't write on your computer screen the way you can on a paper test (though some have tried!), so you have to use the note board they give you, which will be inconveniently located away from the computer screen.

### Scrolling

You have to scroll through Reading Comprehension passages, meaning you won't be able to see an entire passage on the screen at once.

### Elimination

You cannot cross off an answer choice and banish it from your sight (it's on a computer screen, after all), so you have to be disciplined about not reconsidering choices you've already eliminated.

### Strain

Many people find that computer screens tire them and cause eyestrain—especially after four hours.

## KAPLAN STRATEGIES

Kaplan recommends the following CAT Strategies for Test Day:

- **Know the directions cold.** The CAT will switch from one question type to another within a section (going from Reading Comprehension to Sentence Correction, for example) without automatically showing the directions for each new question type. Knowing the format and directions of each GMAT question type beforehand will save you a lot of time—and aggravation—during the exam.

- **Get used to not going back in practice.** Because you won't be able to go back to a previous question on Test Day, get used to this now by practicing in the same way.

- **Get to the difficult stuff quickly.** Because difficult questions are worth more, you want to get to them as soon as possible and to as many of them as possible. That's because right answers on them raise your score a lot, while wrong answers will only lower your score slightly.

- **Pick your battles.** If you cannot answer a question, guess intelligently and move on. There is a hefty penalty for not answering every question in the section, so you need to focus on your pacing. Getting a few stray questions wrong here and there will not hurt your score nearly as much as not getting to all of the questions in the section.

- **Avoid strings of wrong answers.** As you progress through the middle part of the section, individual wrong answers will hurt you slightly (the computer thinks it has found your level), but several wrong answers in a row will sink your score (the computer believes that the current difficulty is completely out of your league). If you know that the previous question you answered was a blind guess, try to get the next one right.

- **Watch out for traps all the time.** Because the level of difficulty of questions on the CAT is not predictable, always be on the lookout for answer-choice traps.

- **Don't sweat the tough stuff!** If the test starts getting hard, that's actually good news because it means that you're doing very well!

## THE SCORE

The GMAT uses an online score-reporting system and consists of the following four scores:

- Overall scaled score of 200–800

- Quantitative scaled subscore of 0–60

- Verbal scaled subscore of 0–60

- Analytical Writing Assessment score of 0–6 (This is separate from your overall score.)

Because the test is graded on a preset curve, the scaled score will correspond to a certain percentile, which will also be given on your score report. A 590 overall score, for instance, corresponds to the 80th percentile, meaning that 80 percent of test takers scored at or below this level. The percentile figure is important, because it allows admissions officers at business schools to get a sense quickly of where you fall in the pool of applicants.

Though many factors play a role in admissions decisions, the GMAT score is usually an important one—and, generally speaking, being average just won't cut it. While the median GMAT score is around 500, you need a score of at least 600 to be considered competitive by the top B-schools. The average GMAT scores at the best business schools in the country—such as Stanford, Sloan (MIT), Kellogg (Northwestern), and Wharton (Penn)—are above 670. That requires besting roughly nine out of every ten test takers!

## THE REPORT

About 20 days after your test date, your official score report will be available online. You'll receive an email when yours is ready. Reports will only be mailed to candidates who request that service. The official score report includes your scores for the Analytical Writing Assessment (AWA), Verbal, and Quantitative sections, as well as your total score and percentile ranking. Test takers who skip the AWA do not receive score reports.

Your report also includes the results of all the exams you've taken in the five years before January 2006, including cancellations. All score-report requests are final and cannot be cancelled.

## THE REGISTRATION

The GMAT is taken by appointment, at your convenience, almost every day of the year. You will be required to register online before making an appointment.

Before you register to take the exam, search for a test center that's convenient for you and determine whether that site has available seats. Each test center operates on its own schedule and can accommodate varying numbers of test takers throughout the day. To locate a test center near you, go to *www.mba.com*.

Available time slots change continuously as people register for the test. You may be able to schedule an appointment within a few days of your desired test date, but popular dates (especially weekends) fill up quickly. You may register and schedule your appointment online, by phone, by mail, or by fax.

When scheduling your test appointment, be sure that the spelling of your name matches the name on the ID you will present at the test center. If those names do not match, you will not be permitted to take the test, and your test fee will be forfeited.

## RESCHEDULING OR CANCELING YOUR TEST DATE

Your exam may be rescheduled for a fee. If you need to reschedule the date, time, or location of your appointment, you may do so for a fee of $50 (at the time of printing) provided that the rescheduling is done at least seven days before the scheduled date. If you need to reschedule and fewer than seven days remain, you will have to pay the full registration amount again. Rescheduling can be done online at *www.mba.com* or by phone. You cannot reschedule an appointment by mail or fax.

Your exam may be cancelled for a partial refund. If you need to cancel your appointment and do so at least seven days before your scheduled date, you will receive an $80 refund (at the time of this book's printing). If you cancel with fewer than seven days remaining, you will forfeit the entire registration fee. For registration fees paid by credit card, the refund amount will be credited to the card. If the fee was paid by check or money order, you will receive a check in the mail. Cancellations can be made online at *www.mba.com* or by phone. You cannot cancel an appointment by mail or fax.

# THE MINDSET

To conquer the test, you must know it. While familiarity with the content is obviously required, many test takers do not realize the stress-fighting power of familiarity with the testing environment itself. To that end, we are providing you with the details of what you can expect on Test Day and how to best prepare your mindset.

## USING THE NOTE BOARD TO YOUR ADVANTAGE

You will be given a spiral-bound note board of laminated paper and a black wet-erase pen. In the United States, Canada, and Mexico, the note board consists of five pale-yellow sheets with numbered legal-sized pages (8.5" × 14") that are spiral-bound at the top. (Paper of a different color may be used outside of these locales.) The first page contains test administration and chair operation instructions and is not suitable for scratch work. Pages 2–10 consist of a gridded work surface. The wet-erase pen is a Staedtler black fine-point.

You will not be given an eraser. The note board is not meant to be reused. Each time you fill up your note board, you can return it to the administrator for a clean one. You may also request a new pen, if necessary. Note boards may not be removed from the testing room at any time, and they must be returned to the administrator upon completion of your exam.

The most efficient way to use your note board is to budget the space for the entire section and only request a replacement between sections. This saves time, as you don't have to wait for the administrator to swap yours before you can continue working. With nine usable pages per note board, this should not be difficult, especially with planning and practice. If you *do* happen to need a new note board (or pen) during a section, hold the used one in the air to clarify immediately the nature of the request (rather than just raising your hand).

With regular practice to build familiarity, most test takers will not have any problems using the note boards and pens on Test Day. However, based on the feedback we've received from test takers, there *are* a couple of snags that you just can't prepare for. Here's how to tackle them:

- **Smudging issues:** If you smudge your work, the best thing to do is simply start over. Think about it: if you continue a futile attempt to save a sinking ship, you will only succeed at wasting your precious time. If you anticipate smudging to be a real issue on Test Day (perhaps due to being left-handed or your writing style), practice often with a dry erase board before Test Day.

- **Pen problems:** If you get a pen that's dry from the start or one that dries out quickly no matter how careful you are with recapping it after use, just get a new pen. If your pen leaves wayward blobs of ink, don't waste time with it either. Ask the administrator for a new pen as soon as it starts to act up.

## MINDSET STRATEGIES

Kaplan recommends the following to prepare your mindset for Test Day.

### Draw a Grid to Eliminate Wrong Answer Choices

If, like most test takers, you find it helpful to cross off answer choices on paper exams, you should do the same on the GMAT. The computer format makes it more of a challenge to pull off, but it can be done with your note board. Because your note board is already gridded, reserve five lines at the top of one of the pages and label them A through E. Use the grid to mark off answer choices that you have eliminated, as shown here.

| A | ✗ | ✗ |   | ✗ |   | ✗ |   |   | ✗ |   | ✗ |   |   |
|---|---|---|---|---|---|---|---|---|---|---|---|---|---|
| B |   | ✗ | ✗ | ✗ |   |   | ✗ | ✗ | ✗ | ✗ |   | ✗ |   |
| C |   |   |   |   | ✗ |   |   |   | ✗ |   |   |   | ✗ |
| D | ✗ |   | ✗ |   | ✗ |   |   | ✗ |   | ✗ |   | ✗ |   |
| E | ✗ | ✗ |   | ✗ |   |   | ✗ |   |   | ✗ |   |   |   |

## Pace Yourself

Running out of time during a section can be a huge blow to both your confidence and your score. To avoid this, you should pace yourself. While you don't need to spend exactly 90 seconds on every Critical Reasoning question, you should try to develop a sense of how much time to spend on each. The best way to do so is to time all of your practice, as that will give you a sense of "how long is too long" by Test Day.

## Hide the Clock If It Distracts You

The timer in the corner of the GMAT screen can work to your advantage, but if you find yourself looking at it so often that it becomes a distraction, turn it off for 10 or 15 minutes and try to refocus. Even if you lose track a bit without the clock, there is no replacement for focus and accuracy.

## Stay Calm

Every standardized test is part psychological warfare between you and the test maker. Losing this mental battle puts you at a severe disadvantage, regardless of your knowledge of the exam's content.

## Mimic Actual Testing Conditions

At Kaplan, we understand the enormous advantage that a stress-free testing environment can provide and how helpful it can be to minimize the differences between practice sessions and Test Day (thereby eliminating the stress). Therefore, we've always recommended that our GMAT students do all of their practice under the same constraints that they would face on the real thing.

Because the note board/pen will be your only option on Test Day, we suggest that you use an eraser board (or anything with a similar surface) and a nonpermanent marker as you work through the material in this book. In fact, Kaplan considers proper stress management to be so important to Test Day success that we provide every classroom course student with practice test experiences that are as close to the actual GMAT as possible—right down to the smallest details, such as giving them a similar note board and a Staedtler black fine-point pen.

When you do practice sets, do them in a quiet room and try them under timed conditions.

## THE PREPARATION

When you've learned the question types and Kaplan strategies and are happy with your performance on practice sets, it's time to use a full-length test as a milestone. Visit *kaptest.com/GMAT* for access to a free full-length practice test.

This book focuses on the most streamlined GMAT strategies, and it is designed to help you prep smarter, not harder. Nevertheless, if you want more coverage of specific Verbal and Quantitative strategies, or more practice sets and tests, we recommend working through Kaplan's GMAT Premier LIVE Online Program. You can find it in stores nationwide or through online retailers.

Realistic practice is essential to a high score on a time-pressured, computer-adaptive exam such as the GMAT, where familiarity with the format leads to increased confidence and improved performance. Kaplan's Ultimate Practice Test is done at an actual GMAT testing site. You do a trial run under actual exam conditions without recording an official score. Experience an actual testing environment firsthand and become familiar with the registration and testing procedures, eliminating Test Day jitters and day-of surprises. Give yourself the competitive advantage! Kaplan's Ultimate Practice Test is available exclusively through GMAT course preparation options. Visit *kaptest.com/GMAT* for more information.

# Part Two

# STREAMLINED REVIEW AND STRATEGIES

# CHAPTER 2: ANALYTICAL WRITING ASSESSMENT

The Analytical Writing Assessment (AWA) tests your ability to analyze a general topic, take an informed position, and write a well-organized, persuasive essay. You will write two essays that are timed separately for 30 minutes each. Topics may be drawn from business or from a wide range of other general interest issues. You will not be required to have any highly technical or specialized knowledge for either essay. You will have basic word processing functions and an area with a scrollbar to type your essays.

## THE SCORE

Each essay is holistically scored on a scale from 0 (worst) to 6 (best) in half-point increments. Each is graded twice—once by a human grader and once by a computer grader known as the e-rater. If the two graders disagree by more than 1 point, a second human grader will have final say on that essay. The scores for both essays are then averaged (rounded up to the nearest half point), and the result will be your AWA score. Most test takers will receive a score between 2 and 6, with 4 being the average.

The following is a table of the general guidelines that AWA graders use.

| Score | Issue Essay | Argument Essay |
|-------|-------------|----------------|
| 6.0 | Demonstrates a keen grasp of all facets of the issue; takes a perceptive position on the issue; uses logical and persuasive evidence to support this position; is tightly focused and well organized; uses language that is descriptive, varied, and precise; contains only minor errors in usage and grammar. | Demonstrates deep understanding of the argument's structure; insightfully identifies and critiques key assumptions; provides compelling support for the critiques; offers ways to improve argument; is tightly focused and well organized; uses language that is descriptive, varied, and precise; contains only minor errors. |
| 5.0 | Demonstrates clear and in-depth understanding of the issue; presents a thoughtful position on the issue; uses relevant examples to support the position; is focused and organized; language and sentence structure are clear and have some variety; contains only minor errors in usage and grammar. | Demonstrates clear grasp of the argument's structure; understands key assumptions; critique is based on examining validity of assumptions; is focused and organized; language and sentence structure are clear and have some variety; contains only minor errors in usage and grammar. |
| 4.0 | Demonstrates a basic ability to grasp and take a position on the issue; position on the issue is clear; most if not all evidence is relevant; focus and organization are strong enough to avoid detracting from the argument; conveys meaning with clarity; contains no major errors in grammar, usage, or mechanics. | Demonstrates competence in analysis and writing; identifies evidence and conclusions; critique is based on assessment of assumptions; focus and organization are strong enough to avoid detracting from the argument; conveys meaning with clarity; contains no major errors in grammar, usage, or mechanics. |
| 3.0 | Demonstrates some understanding of the issue but has clear weaknesses, including at least one of the following: position on the issue (if any is stated) is superficial or imprecise, evidence is often not cogent, organization and focus are inconsistent, language does not convey meaning with clarity; contains some major errors in standard written English or frequent minor errors. | Demonstrates some capacity for analysis but has conspicuous shortcomings, including at least one of the following: fails to identify evidence and conclusion clearly, fails to address some key assumptions, critique is illogical or tangential, organization and focus are inconsistent, language does not convey meaning with clarity; contains some major errors in standard written English or frequent minor errors. |

| 2.0 | Demonstrates a very limited capacity for analytical writing; discussion of and position on the issue (if any) lacks depth, clarity, and insight; evidence (if any) is generally not compelling or relevant; provides little organization or structure; problems with language, grammar, and sentence structure are severe and/or persistent. | Demonstrates only a limited ability to analyze an argument; does not show grasp of argument's structure; analysis based more on personal opinion than on a logical critique of assumptions; provides little organization or structure; problems with language, grammar, and sentence structure are severe and/or persistent. |
|---|---|---|
| 1.0 | Demonstrates a near-total lack of analytical writing competence; shows little or no understanding of the issue—or does not even address the issue; is unfocused, unstructured, disorganized; has major errors in grammar, language, and sentence structure that greatly obscure the writer's meaning. | Demonstrates lack of ability to conduct analysis and write clearly; shows little or no understanding of the argument's evidence, conclusion, or assumptions—or does not even address the argument; is unfocused, unstructured, and disorganized; has major errors in grammar, language, and sentence structure that greatly obscure the writer's meaning. |

# THE STRATEGY

Before we review the specific strategies for each of the two types of essays, it's worth noting the following general strategies for the section:

- **Organization:** Always plan out your essay with an outline before you begin writing. A properly outlined essay makes it much harder for the writer to lose his or her train of thought midparagraph, and the end result will be much easier for both graders to follow along.

- **Structure:** The e-rater can't judge creativity, so a structured—even formulaic— approach to writing essays is essential.

- **Style:** Vary the structure of your sentences. Human and computer graders alike will appreciate it.

- **Transition:** Use transitional phrases, such as *first, therefore, because,* and *for example,* so that the computer can recognize the structure of your argument.

- **Syntax:** Avoid misspellings and grammatical errors. While the e-rater won't lower your grade for the occasional misspelling, it might misinterpret the misspelled word as something you did not mean to say.

- **Variety:** Use synonyms for important terms, because the computer views them as indicators of a strong vocabulary and a wide range of knowledge. For example, if your essay is about promoting a product, be sure to include synonyms for the word *promotion,* such as *advertising, marketing, publicity,* and so on. You should also include pertinent, specific examples of promotional campaigns.

- **Format:** Use the standards of logical analysis whenever possible. When critiquing an argument, analyze the strength of the evidence presented, point out unwarranted assumptions, and present neglected alternatives. When constructing your own argument, make your points of evidence specific and defensible, avoid unwarranted assumptions, and anticipate your opposition by providing a refutation of the strongest point against your own argument.

Let's explore the two types of essays individually and see how best to attack them.

# ANALYSIS OF AN ARGUMENT

For your first essay, you'll be required to analyze and critique an argument. The following instruction and prompt screens are the same ones you'll see on Test Day. It's important to note that the timer starts when you see the first screen, so knowing these cold will save you time on the actual GMAT.

**Screen 1: General Instructions Analytical Writing Assessment Instructions**

> **Analysis of an Argument Essay**
> **Time: 30 Minutes**
>
> In this part of the test, you will be asked to write a critical analysis of the argument in the prompt. You are not being asked to give your own views on the topic.
>
> **COMPOSING YOUR ESSAY:** Before you begin to type, take a little time to look at the argument and plan your essay. Make sure your ideas are organized and clearly stated. Leave some time to read over your essay and make any changes you think are necessary. You will have 30 minutes to write your essay.

**ESSAY ASSESSMENT:** Qualified graders with varied backgrounds, including experience in business subject areas, will assess the overall quality of your analysis and composition. They will look at how well you

- identify key elements of the argument and examine them;
- arrange your analysis of the argument presented;
- give appropriate examples and reasons for support; and
- master the components of written English.

### Screen 2: Specific Prompt

Read the argument and the directions that follow it, and write down any ideas that will be helpful in mapping out your essay. Begin writing your essay in the box at the bottom of this screen.

*[The unique argument you will write about will appear here.]*

Consider how logical you find this argument. In your essay, be sure to discuss the line of reasoning and the use of evidence in the argument. For example, you may need to consider what questionable assumptions underlie the thinking and what alternative explanations or counterpoints might weaken the conclusion. You may also discuss what types of evidence would strengthen or refute the argument, what changes in the argument would make it more logically sound, and what, if anything, would help you better evaluate its conclusion.

Let's examine the components in more detail.

## THE DIRECTIONS

The directions wisely advise you to plan out your essay before writing anything. In this type of essay, that involves taking a few minutes to identify the conclusion, the evidence, and any assumptions that the author has made (there are bound to be a few). Then spend five minutes organizing these points into an essay before you start typing.

## THE STIMULUS

Much like Critical Reasoning arguments, the author will try to sell you on a particular point of view through his or her evidence. The key to critiquing the argument correctly lies in spotting his or her underlying assumptions (unstated information that is needed to prove the conclusion).

## THE QUESTION

The question stem wants to know how convincing you find the argument. Arguments in these prompts will always be flawed, and it will be up to you to explain why in your essay.

# THE METHOD

To critique an argument properly, you must attack it as forcefully as possible. Because these arguments will require unstated assumptions to connect evidence logically to the conclusion, the best way to attack them is to go after those assumptions.

## THE "LAUNDRY LIST" FORMAT

The laundry list format requires you to make a list of all the assumptions and logical errors in the argument *before* you start writing. Your goal is to show that you understand the argument in your introduction, dissect the issues in your body paragraphs, and show that you can "repair" the argument in your conclusion.

1. **Introduction Paragraph**

   - Restate the conclusion to be evaluated.

   - Restate the given evidence.

   - Declare that the argument is not persuasive due to serious gaps between evidence and conclusion.

2. **Body Paragraph(s)**

   - Identify a key assumption or logical error.

   - Explain how you can weaken the assumption or why the logic does not follow.

3. **Concluding Paragraph**

   - Boldly reaffirm your stance.

   - Explain how the argument could be strengthened.

# SAMPLE PROMPT

Let's try evaluating some essays. Have a look at the following sample prompt:

> Read the argument and the directions that follow it, and write down any ideas that will be helpful in mapping out your essay. Begin writing your essay in the box at the bottom of this screen.
>
> The following appeared on the editorial page of a local newspaper:
>
> The government should not attempt to aid unproductive farmers by inflating prices. When prices are high, it is possible for farmers to use inefficient methods of production and still generate a profit. The progress of farming technology is stalled, and farmers remain dependent on artificially inflated pricing.
>
> Consider how logical you find this argument. In your essay, be sure to discuss the line of reasoning and the use of evidence in the argument. For example, you may need to consider what questionable assumptions underlie the thinking and what alternative explanations or counterpoints might weaken the conclusion. You may also discuss what types of evidence would strengthen or refute the argument, what changes in the argument would make it more logically sound, and what, if anything, would help you better evaluate its conclusion.

Good GMAT essay writers will take a few minutes to break down the argument. What did you think was the **conclusion**? What **evidence** did the author use? What **unstated assumptions** tied the conclusion to the evidence?

If you were writing a response to this question, how would you have critiqued the argument? Think of this when you judge the following two essays, each of which tries to analyze the above argument.

## SAMPLE ARGUMENT RESPONSE 1:

It is hard to conclude what is being concluded here since the author doesn't necessarily back it up all the way. We know what teh government shouldn't do, and we pretty much know why. If prices are high, then farmers dont use good methods of production. They still make money, though. Then progress don't go forward, and farmers get hooked on inflation of prices, much like in the old saying that if you give someone a fish, then they are dependent on you, but if you teach them to fish, then they are free forever.

So we are shown that its a bad idea to make inflated pricing, and the government shouldn't be doing it. No problem, except that why should we beleive it? Maybe what he says isn't true, and the farmers are doing something different. Maybe they are just pretending to need higher prices, and they're puting all their money into cars or drugs or even super-speed tractors, which actually cancels out the part about the tecnology, because if they could afford those, then they don't need the government's money from them. Also, maybe the farmers use really good methods, then just take time off. We just don't know what's happening in between the chunks that the author gives us, behind the scenes, and we don't know whether he can be believed.

To make me believe it, I would need to be told that all of or lots of these farmers need the money, and aren't using fancy mashinery, and therefore shouldn't be given what they want from the government because it's not good for them in the long run, because they're adicted to it and they can't get away and things just get worse with the tecnology. If I could beleive all of that, if the author told me enough to make me beleive it, then it would be a very good argument.

## SAMPLE ARGUMENT RESPONSE 2:

The author concludes in the first sentence that it's a bad idea for the government to inflate prices for farm products. As evidence for her conclusion, she explains that high prices allow farmers to use poor production methods and still make money. This keeps farm technology from improving and thus ties farmers to the artificial pricing. So artificially high prices lead to inefficient methods, which leads to a lack of progress, which leads to dependence on artificial pricing. Indeed, this chain of evidence does seem to make it clear that the government shouldn't inflate prices on farm products. If we accept that the scenario described by the evidence is accurate, then the argument is quite convincing. But the argument becomes far less convincing if we examine the author's assumptions.

First, she says that artificial pricing makes it "possible" for farmers to use inefficient methods. However, she doesn't provide evidence to show that even though it is possible most or even any farmers would behave in this manner. It is even arguable that farmers would use the extra money to invest in advanced technology. This possibility seems to call this key evidence into question by undermining the assumption that farmers, if given the opportunity, will use inefficient production methods.

In addition, the author assumes that the farmers are dependent on the artificial pricing—that they are just taking it easy because they know that government pricing protects them. Given the nature of farming, these tariffs might be needed to protect farmers from occasional natural disasters beyond their control, events such as floods, or drought. That a bad year might force the farmers to go out of business altogether if unprotected by higher tariffs is not considered by the author.

As mentioned above, this argument is convincing if one can believe that the evidence presented is correct. Some of the assumptions linking the various pieces of evidence, however, are quite easy to undermine without additional "proof" in the form of evidence. To make this argument more persuasive, I would look for facts to back up the author's assertions, perhaps statistics that show how quickly farming technology has developed during periods when artificially inflated pricing was in effect. Information about individual farm communities and the effect that pricing has on their production and economic standing would also be helpful in making an evaluation of the validity of the conclusion. Overall, while the evidence seems to form a solid structure of support for the conclusion of this argument, the author should seek additional facts to strengthen her chain of unsupported assumptions.

## How Would You Score These Essays?

Take a moment to evaluate them using the AWA Scoring Scale on page 20. When you are ready, compare your reasoning to our analysis at the end of this chapter on page 33.

# ANALYSIS OF AN ISSUE

Your second essay, Analysis of an Issue, presents two different viewpoints regarding a specific issue. After choosing one of the views, you are to write an essay that shows why the side you chose is the correct one. The instruction and prompt screens that follow are the same ones you'll see on the GMAT. As with the Analysis of an Argument screens, knowing these cold will save you time on Test Day.

### Screen 1: General Instructions

Analytical Writing Assessment Instructions
Analysis of an Issue Essay
Time: 30 Minutes

In this part of the test, you are asked to explain your views on the issue presented. There is no "right" answer. Rather, you should take into consideration multiple viewpoints as you put together your own position on the issue.

**COMPOSING YOUR ESSAY:** Read the issue and the directions that follow it. Before you start to type, take a little time to think about the issue, plan your essay, and take notes that will help you. Make sure to flesh out and organize your ideas, but leave time to read over your essay and make any necessary edits. You will have 30 minutes to write your essay.

**ESSAY ASSESSMENT:** Qualified graders with varied backgrounds, including experience in business subject areas, will assess the overall quality of your analysis and composition. They will look at how well you

- explore your ideas and develop a position on the issue;
- arrange your argument around the issue presented;
- give appropriate examples and reasons for support; and
- master the components of written English.

**Screen 2: Specific Prompt**

> Read the statement and the instructions that follow it and then take notes that will help you plan your response.
>
> *[The unique argument you will write about will appear here.]*
>
> To what extent do you agree or disagree with (a position from the prompt will appear here)? Explain your positions using relevant reasons and/or examples from your own experience, observations, or reading.

Let's examine the components in more detail.

## THE DIRECTIONS

The directions wisely advise you to plan out your essay before writing anything. In this type of essay, begin by digesting the issue, brainstorming ideas, and choosing a side. Then spend a few minutes selecting the points you will make and organizing them into an essay before you start typing.

## THE STIMULUS

The first sentence or two of the stimulus introduces a general "issue" and expresses a view on it. If two viewpoints are expressed, there may or may not be a keyword—such as *but, however,* or *yet*—to signal the introduction of a contrasting point of view. The last part of the stimulus will usually discuss the opposing view. Prior knowledge of specific subject matters won't be needed.

## THE QUESTION

The stem will instruct you to take a position on the issue and explain why you prefer that position. In addition to developing a clear line of reasoning, you will also need to back up your assertions with examples. It is not enough to simply say why you like your position: you must also say why it is preferable to opposing points of view.

# THE METHOD

The key to a compelling issue analysis is to be decisive. Boldly choose a side and defend it well while attacking the weaknesses of opposing positions. The following format will enable you to do this in a clear, cogent, and concise manner.

## THE "WINNER/LOSER" FORMAT

The ability to create a short, tight analysis of the issue at hand is far better than the ability to type in more words than other test takers use. Remember, you aren't judged on how much you write.

1. **Introduction Paragraph**

   - Restate the issue in your own terms.

   - Define any ambiguous terms.

   - Declare the position you will take on the issue.

2. **Body Paragraph**

   - Argue your position with specific points of argument.

   - Support your claims with reasons and/or examples.

   - Address weaknesses of your position. (Place in a separate paragraph if lengthy.)

3. **Concluding Paragraph**

   - Refute opposing positions.

   - Attack their strengths and expose their weaknesses.

   - Boldly reaffirm your stance.

# SAMPLE PROMPT

Look at the following sample prompt:

> Read the statement and the instructions that follow it and then take notes that will help you plan your response.
>
> "Some people argue that those who do not send their children to public schools should not have to fund these schools through taxes, since neither they nor their children benefit from these schools. They ignore the fact that everyone benefits from the strong economy that a well-educated populace generates."
>
> Which argument do you find more compelling, the case for forcing everyone to fund public schools or the opposing viewpoint? Explain your position using relevant reasons and/or examples from your own experience, observations, or reading.

Which points would *you* present to either argue for or against public school funding? Consider that as you evaluate the following two essays.

## SAMPLE ISSUE RESPONSE 1:

The author concludes that people who argue that those who do not send their children to public schools should not have to fund those schools through their taxes, since neither they nor their children benefit from these schools, ignore the fact that everyone benefits from the strong economy that a well-educated public generates. If students don't go to public school, then they go somewhere else instead, like a private school, or maybe they're taught at home. That means that the selfs are already taking care of the kid's education, unless of course the person doesn't even have children. In any case, they're being asked to pay for a service they're not using. How would you like it if you didn't own a phone, but still got a phone bill every month, or if you had to pay rent even though you own your own home? This is obviously unfair. But actually it's not as unfair as you think. It's unfair that people who don't have a lot of money shouldn't be able to send their kids to good schools.

Besides, everyone benefits from the strong economy that a well-educated populace generates. And how are you going to have a well-educated populace without public schools? What this means is that even though it's not fair to have to pay for something you don't use, people who don't send their children to public schools should still fund these schools through their taxes. It's just the right thing to do.

## Sample Issue Response 2:

The author concludes that all taxpayers—even those with no school-age children, or those whose children are schooled outside of the public school system—should be required to help fund the public schools. The author refutes critics of this view by noting that a well-educated populace contributes to a strong economy, and that a strong economy in turn benefits all, including adults with no children in public school, and children who do not go to public school. As I shall demonstrate, this argument is correct.

First, the author is right in saying that a strong economy requires a generally high level of education. Over the past several decades, most jobs in heavy industry have moved overseas, resulting in a sharp reduction of remunerative job opportunities for anyone without a college degree. Strong primary and secondary schooling is therefore needed to allow people to become qualified for those jobs. Moreover, the absence of a well-educated, employable populace has a negative impact on society, in the form of crime, substance abuse, and the decay of local infrastructures, all of which are associated with ill-educated (and therefore poor) communities, and all of which contribute to the collapse of the local economy and the reduction of educational and employment opportunities.

Although it may appear to be an unwarranted assumption that only a heavily funded public school system can supply the instruction needed to create a well-educated populace, the fact is that the alternatives to public school—for example, privates schools, parochial schools, and home schooling—can only accommodate a minority of students. For the majority, including many of those whom poverty, learning disabilities, or other adverse circumstances have placed at the greatest risk of leaving school, public schools provide the only guarantee of an education.

The contrary argument is that people who do not send their children to public schools do not benefit (and their children do not benefit) from these schools. This argument confuses school taxes with tuition: it supposes that taxes for public programs are fees for use. We require taxpayers to support foreign aid, space exploration—all kinds of things that they don't use directly. Yet they often benefit from these things indirectly, as a person who doesn't drive may benefit from the commerce facilitated by publicly funded highways. The person whose children go to private schools may one day be treated by a doctor who was taught at a public school. Thus, a well-funded public school systems benefits everyone.

### How Would You Score These Essays?

Take a moment to evaluate them using the AWA Scoring Scale on page 20. When you are ready, compare your reasoning to our analysis starting on page 36.

# THE WRAP-UP

The Analytical Writing Assessment can be just as predictable as the other sections of the test if approached with the right plan. A well-written essay pays special attention to *organization, structure, style, transition, syntax, variety,* and *format.*

The Analysis of an Argument requires exploring the given argument's *underlying assumptions* and *logical errors.* The Analysis of an Issue involves *defending your side* and *attacking the opposing positions.*

# SAMPLE ARGUMENT ESSAYS EXPLAINED

Turn to page 25 to have another look at the Sample Argument Prompt.

## KAPLAN'S ANALYSIS: SAMPLE ARGUMENT RESPONSE 1

Turn to page 26 to reread the Sample Argument Response 1.

The redundant opening sentence—"It is hard to conclude what is being concluded here"—is a clear sign that the writer is having trouble identifying the key components of the original argument. At times, he does seem to have a sense of the argument's conclusion, evidence, and assumptions, but it is very difficult to tell whether he is or isn't aware of the argument's structure because he does not explicitly state these terms.

In the second paragraph, the writer tries to identify some of the weaknesses in the argument. However, because he was not clear about the topic of the original argument, his point ends up being a tangent about what the farmers do with government subsidies.

In his final paragraph, the author tries to recommend a way to strengthen the argument he is critiquing. He suggests that the argument would be stronger if it were proven that government money stops the progress of farm technology. However, the author does not state this point clearly, and he weakens his point with irrelevant observations about the farmers' need for the money.

The essay is poorly organized, though the writer did try to impose some structure.

Paragraph 1: A (poor) analysis of the argument's structure and conclusion

Paragraph 2: A (confused) discussion of the author's assumptions

Paragraph 3: Overall weaknesses and strengths of the argument

While this poorly written essay reveals a weak grasp of the argument at hand, there is some evidence that the writer tried to organize his thoughts. Even poorly argued essays can benefit from well-organized paragraphs.

You could argue that the use of language was certainly original, but GMAT graders like things to be clear and correct. The clumsy expressions found throughout this essay, as well as the consistently poor spelling and grammar ("hard to conclude what is being concluded," "progress don't go forward," and "if I could beleive all that, if the author told me enough to beleive it"), significantly lower our score estimate for this essay. While graders will overlook the occasional mistake, an abundance of errors will negatively impact your score. Be sure to save time to proofread your essay at the end.

**Final Score:** 1

## KAPLAN'S ANALYSIS: SAMPLE ARGUMENT RESPONSE 2:

Turn to page 26 to reread the Sample Argument Response 2.

The writer explicitly states the main features of the argument with "The author concludes. . ." and "As evidence for her conclusion. . ." in the first paragraph. She then goes on to restate the chain of events that the stimulus proposes, clarifying the original argument. Paragraphs 2 and 3 address the author's assumptions. Note that the writer wisely chose to express the conclusion and evidence in her own words rather than simply restating what was presented in the prompt.

Using the laundry list format, the writer devoted a short paragraph to each of the two refutable assumptions she discovered to attack the argument. As an added bonus, she also identified an ambiguous term in the stimulus: when prices are high, it is *possible* for farmers to use inefficient methods. In this case, *possibility* does not necessarily mean *certainty*. Identifying shifts in logic based on ambiguous terms can be a very effective tactic in attacking an argument.

In the final paragraph, the writer explains how the argument could be strengthened. Notice that she doesn't simply say that the assumptions must be true—she gives specific examples of the types of evidence needed to support them. This practical advice makes the argument much more concrete, which will lead to a higher score on the essay.

The essay is clear and well organized.

Paragraph 1: Here's the argument and I don't like it.

Paragraph 2: The first reason I don't like it—an unwarranted assumption

Paragraph 3: The second reason I don't like it—another unwarranted assumption

Paragraph 4: Here's how it could have been improved.

The use of language is correct, but the essay is a bit long and some of it wordy. Overall, however, this is a fairly minor quibble. There were no major grammatical errors.

**Final Score:** 6

# SAMPLE ISSUE ESSAYS EXPLAINED

Turn to page 31 to have another look at the Sample Issue Prompt.

## KAPLAN'S ANALYSIS: SAMPLE ARGUMENT RESPONSE 1

Turn to page 31 to reread the Sample Issue Response 1.

The writer may have identified the issue to be analyzed, but she failed to show it clearly in this essay. The essay begins by repeating the stimulus practically word for word. This does not demonstrate to the grader that the writer has grasped the issue as well as paraphrasing would. An essay that repeats large chunks of the stimulus feels hollow and tells the grader that the writer does not know what's going on.

The writer does not defend a position: she seems to agree with both sides! The essay begins by supporting the idea that people shouldn't be taxed for an education that neither they nor their children receive. The writer defends her position using the phone bill example. However, instead of sticking with this position, she then goes on to support the opposing viewpoint. This results in a confusing mishmash of ideas. The key to writing a strong issue analysis is to pick a clear side and stick with it. The only wrong choice in this type of essay is not making one!

The strongest part of this essay would most likely be the examples of unfair situations that are analogous to paying for an education you do not receive. The phone bill and rent examples are concrete, real-world examples that can make a compelling argument. Unfortunately, the essay itself does not present a coherent argument.

The essay's primary weakness is its extremely poor organization. The writer had good ideas, but her failure to delineate separate points of argument caused them to be lost in the mess. The main problem is the lack of paragraphs to split the essay into bite-sized pieces. Proper use of paragraphs is essential to a strong essay. The advantage of Kaplan's winner/loser format is that it forces you to think and plan in paragraphs.

The use of language was, for the most part, correct. However, the sentences did tend to run on, and the whole essay would have been more coherent if shorter, clearer sentences were used. There were no major grammatical errors.

**Final Score:** 2

## KAPLAN'S ANALYSIS: SAMPLE ARGUMENT RESPONSE 2

Turn to page 32 to reread the Sample Issue Response 2.

In the first paragraph, the issue is restated in the writer's own words, and he clearly chooses a side. The prose is direct and to the point, and the writer does not waste time on extraneous information.

The writer offers a number of relevant examples to help his case and clarify his points. The last three paragraphs all contain examples that make the argument clearer. The examples of poverty and learning disabilities in the third paragraph clearly illustrate the adverse circumstances he mentions. In the final paragraph, he gives a strong example—a publicly educated doctor treating a privately educated patient—that supports his entire position.

This essay is clear and well organized.

Paragraph 1: Here's the issue and the position I take on it.

Paragraph 2: Here's evidence for why my position is correct.

Paragraph 3: Here's why criticism of my position is incorrect.

Paragraph 4: Here's why other positions are misguided plus a short affirmation of my correctness.

The use of language was correct and varied. The sentences varied in length, but all were fairly straightforward and to the point. Vocabulary was varied as well. For instance, rather than reusing the word *education* over and over, the writer replaces it with *schooling, teaching,* and *instruction.*

There were no major grammatical errors.

**Final Score:** 6

# CHAPTER 3: **PROBLEM SOLVING**

Problem Solving questions are standard multiple-choice math problems consisting of a question followed by five answer choices, one of which is correct. They are the classic math problems found on many standardized tests, so you should be somewhat familiar with this question type. Problem Solving questions primarily focus on high school-level arithmetic, algebra, and geometry.

Of the 37 questions in the Quantitative section, roughly 22 of them are of the Problem Solving variety, so your performance on these questions will largely determine your Quantitative subscore. The directions will look something like this:

> **Directions:** Solve the problem and choose the best answer.
>
> Notes:
>
> 1. All numbers used are real numbers.
> 2. Figures are drawn as accurately as possible unless otherwise noted.
> 3. Lines shown are straight whether they appear straight or jagged.
> 4. Points, angles, regions, etc. exist in the order shown.
> 5. Angle measurements are positive.
> 6. All figures lie in a plane unless noted otherwise.

## THE DIRECTIONS

The directions are pretty straightforward: solve the problem and choose the best answer out of the choices given.

## The Notes

The notes are here to make your life easier by closing up "what if" loopholes. Numbers aren't imaginary, figures consist of straight lines, and things are as they appear unless otherwise noted.

## The Questions

Problem Solving questions are usually pretty straightforward. They are often presented as "word problems"—short-story situations that require you to conceptualize mathematically. Each question comes with five choices, only one of which is correct. If you cannot figure out the correct answer, eliminating choices will greatly improve your odds of guessing correctly.

Here is a typical Problem Solving question:

1. A car rental company charges $x$ dollars per mile for the first $n$ miles and $x + 1$ dollars per mile for each additional mile. How much will the mileage charge be, in dollars, for a journey of $d$ miles, where $d > n$?

   ○ $d(x + 1) - n$
   ○ $xn + d$
   ○ $xn + d(x + 1)$
   ○ $x(n + d) + d$
   ○ $(x + 1)(d - n)$

# THE STRATEGY

For many test takers, the mistake they make is thinking that the Quantitative section is a math test. While the GMAT certainly tests your knowledge of basic math concepts, the focus of this section is actually on your *critical thinking skills* with the concepts that you know.

Because a critical thinking test focuses more on how well you think, rather than how well you compute, the best way to tackle this section of the test is to *find the quickest and least error-prone solution to a problem*, which does not always involve slogging through the math.

This chapter focuses on two of Kaplan's proven strategies designed to help you critically think your way to the correct answers on Problem Solving questions using minimal math: picking numbers and back-solving.

## PICKING NUMBERS

Which of the following questions would you rather see on Test Day?

2. Seven years from now, Carlos will be twice as old as his sister Anita will be then. If Carlos is now $C$ years old, how many years old is Anita?

   ○ $\dfrac{C-7}{2}$

   ○ $C - 7$

   ○ $\dfrac{C+7}{2}$

   ○ $\dfrac{2C-7}{2}$

   ○ $2C - 7$

3. Seven years from now, Carlos will be twice as old as his sister Anita will be then. If Carlos is now 13 years old, how many years old is Anita?

   ○ 3

   ○ 6

   ○ 9.5

   ○ 10

   ○ 19

The correct answer to both questions is **(A)**. While the math in the two questions is identical, the use of a quantity (13) in question 3 instead of a variable **(C)** in question 2 makes the former a lot more concrete—and therefore easier.

This is the principle behind what makes picking numbers so useful. The picking numbers strategy really shines when

1.  there are variables in the question stem and the answer choices; and/or

2.  when a percent, fraction, or ratio problem contains no actual values.

### Kaplan's 4-Step Method for Picking Numbers

For many GMAT test takers, what makes Problem Solving questions difficult is not so much the math itself as the confusion that an abundance of variables can create. Because these variables are really the main (and sometimes only) reason why the questions seem hard in the first place, use the picking numbers strategy to remove this obstacle. The idea is to make the problem as concrete as possible by replacing all of its confusing variables.

> **Step 1: Pick numbers that are *permissible* and *manageable* to stand in for the variables.**
>
> **Step 2: Answer the question using the number(s) you picked.**
>
> **Step 3: Plug your numbers into each of the five choices, eliminating those that give a different result.**
>
> **Step 4: Repeat steps 1–3 with a different set of numbers if more than one choice remains.**

*Permissible* and *manageable* simply mean that the number must make sense in accordance with the question itself and be a number you can work with. For example, while you *could* pick a number like 35,927, doing so would only make life difficult. Let's look at this in more detail with the following examples:

4.  If $a > 1$, what is the value of $\dfrac{2a+6}{a^2+2a-3}$ ?

    ○ $a$

    ○ $a + 3$

    ○ $\dfrac{2}{a-1}$

    ○ $\dfrac{2a}{a-3}$

    ○ $\dfrac{a-1}{2}$

**Step 1: Pick numbers that are *permissible* and *manageable* to stand in for the variables.** Because the question states that $a > 1$, you wouldn't (and shouldn't) pick a number such as -1. That is *not* permissible. However, because a > 1 is our *only* restriction, let's use a very manageable number for $a$, $a = 2$.

**Step 2: Answer the question using the number(s) you picked.** Substituting 2 for $a$ in the fraction gives us

$$\frac{2a+6}{a^2+2a-3} = \frac{2(2)+6}{2^2+2(2)-3} = \frac{4+6}{4+4-3} = \frac{10}{5} = 2$$

Therefore, when $a = 2$, the value of the fraction is also 2.

**Step 3: Plug your numbers into each of the five choices, eliminating those that give a different result.** Plug 2 in for $a$ in each of the five choices to see which one(s) produce a result of 2:

**(A)**, $a$, is correct so keep it.

**(B)**, $a + 3 = 2 + 3 = 5$, so eliminate this choice.

**(C)**, $\dfrac{2}{a-1} = \dfrac{2}{2-1} = 2$, so keep this choice.

**(D)**, $\dfrac{2a}{a-3} = \dfrac{2(2)}{2-3} = -4$, so eliminate it.

**(E)**, $\dfrac{a-1}{2} = \dfrac{2-1}{2} = 0.5$, so eliminate it.

**Step 4: Repeat steps 1–3 with a different set of numbers if more than one choice remains.** **(A)** and **(C)** remain, so pick a different number to test them both. Let's try $a = 3$.

Substituting 3 for $a$ in the fraction gives us

$$\frac{2a+6}{a^2+2a-3} = \frac{2(3)+6}{3^2+2(3)-3} = \frac{6+6}{9+6-3} = \frac{12}{12} = 1$$

Therefore, when $a = 3$, the value of the fraction is 1.

Plug 3 in for $a$ in each remaining choice to see which one(s) produce a result of 1:

○ $a$

○ $\cancel{a+3}$

○ $\dfrac{2}{a-1}$

○ $\dfrac{\cancel{2a}}{\cancel{a-3}}$

○ $\dfrac{\cancel{a-1}}{\cancel{2}}$

**(A)** does not give you a value of 1 when $a = 3$, so it can be eliminated. That leaves **(C)** as the correct answer.

Now, let's look at some more sample questions where picking numbers is the best strategy of attack.

5.  The value of a certain stock rose by 30 percent from March to April, then decreased by 20 percent from April to May. The stock's value in May was what percent of its value in March?

    ○ 90%

    ○ 104%

    ○ 110%

    ○ 150%

    ○ 156%

**Step 1: Pick numbers that are *permissible* and *manageable* to stand in for the variables.** While the problem is about the value of a stock, the actual value is never given. Because this problem deals with percents (which are parts of 100), the best number to pick is always 100.

**Step 2: Answer the question using the number(s) you picked.** Our volatile stock rises 30 percent before dropping 20 percent. Because we picked 100 for the starting price, a 30 percent rise is an increase of $100 \times 30\% = 30$ for a new stock price of $100 + 30 = 130$. At a price of 130, the stock drops 20 percent, or $130 \times 20\% = 26$

for a final stock price of 130 − 26 = 104. Because we started with an initial price of 100, the stock is 104 percent of its original value. That's **(B)**, so no further steps are necessary.

6. At a certain international function, $\frac{1}{5}$ of the people attending were male Greek citizens. If the number of female Greek citizens attending was $\frac{2}{3}$ greater than the number of male Greek citizens attending, what fraction of the people at the dinner were not Greek citizens?

- ○ $\frac{1}{5}$
- ○ $\frac{2}{5}$
- ○ $\frac{7}{15}$
- ○ $\frac{8}{15}$
- ○ $\frac{2}{3}$

**Step 1: Pick numbers that are *permissible* and *manageable* to stand in for the variables.** This problem does not have any variables, but that doesn't mean you can't pick numbers. The function attendees are represented by fractional values, so pick a number for the total number of attendees.

In Problem Solving questions involving fractions, the best total number to pick is the least common multiple (LCM) of the denominators in the five choices. In this problem, that's 15.

**Step 2: Answer the question using the number(s) you picked.** You know that $\frac{1}{5}$ of the 15 total attendees were male Greek citizens, so there were $\frac{1}{5} \times 15 = 3$ male Greek citizens. The number of female Greek citizens was $\frac{2}{3} \times 3 = 2$ greater than this, so there were 3 + 2 = 5 female Greek citizens. This brings the total number of Greek citizens to 3 + 5 = 8, leaving 15 − 8 = 7 attendees who aren't Greek citizens. We chose 15 as our whole, so the fraction is $\frac{7}{15}$, or **(C)**.

Let's look again at the question from the beginning of this chapter.

7. A car rental company charges $x$ dollars per mile for the first $n$ miles and $x + 1$ dollars per mile for each additional mile. How much will the mileage charge be, in dollars, for a journey of $d$ miles, where $d > n$?

- ○ $d(x + 1) - n$
- ○ $xn + d$
- ○ $xn + d(x + 1)$
- ○ $x(n + d) + d$
- ○ $(x + 1)(d - n)$

**Step 1: Pick numbers that are *permissible* and *manageable* to stand in for the variables.** While you might be tempted to choose a very reasonable rate, such as 25¢ per mile for the first 200 miles, such realistic choices will only serve to make the math more difficult than it needs to be. The expressions in the answer choices look rather complicated, so let's keep our numbers small. Try $x = 2$, $n = 3$, and $d = 4$.

**Step 2: Answer the question using the number(s) you picked.** Substituting the values into the problem results in the following:

The first three miles cost $2 per mile for a charge of $3 \times 2 = \$6$. The final mile costs $2 + 1 = \$3$ per mile for a charge of $3 \times 1 = \$3$. Therefore, the total charge is $6 + 3 = \$9$.

**Step 3: Plug your numbers into each of the five choices, eliminating those that give a different result.** Plug 2 in for $x$, 3 in for $n$, and 4 in for $d$ into each of the five choices to see which one(s) produce a result of 9:

**(A)**, $d(x + 1) - n$ is $4(2 + 1) - 3 = 4(3) - 3 = 12 - 3 = 9$, so keep this.

**(B)**, $xn + d$ is $2(3) + 4 = 6 + 4 = 10$. Therefore, you can eliminate this choice.

**(C)**, $xn + d(x + 1)$ is $2(3) + 4(2 + 1) = 6 + 4(3) = 6 + 12 = 18$, so you can eliminate this.

**(D)**, $x(n + d) + d$ is $2(3 + 4) + 4 = 2(7) + 4 = 14 + 4 = 18$. Therefore, eliminate this.

**(E)**, $(x + 1)(d - n)$ is $(2 + 1)(4 - 3) = 3(1) = 3$. Therefore, you can eliminate this choice.

Only **(A)** produces a result of 9, so it must be correct.

## BACK-SOLVING

What makes the following question difficult?

8. Employee *X* is paid $12.50 an hour no matter how many hours he works per week. Employee *Y* is paid $10 an hour for the first 30 hours she works in a week and 1.5 times that for each additional hour. On a certain week, both employees worked the same number of hours and were paid the same amount. How many hours did each employee work that week?

- ◯ 48
- ◯ 50
- ◯ 54
- ◯ 60
- ◯ 64

Well, for starters, solving it using algebra will require some really messy math to say the least. You *could* do it that way, but do you *really* want to spend *that* much time on a question under the GMAT's time constraints (not to mention the likelihood of making a mistake when that amount of math is involved)? Furthermore, unfortunately, there doesn't seem to be any way to pick numbers either.

The key to solving this problem without pulling your hair out lies in the simplicity of the answer choices—each is simply a number. While you do not know which is correct, you *do* know that it must be one of the five. Such a scenario calls for back-solving.

### Kaplan's 3-Step Method for Back-solving

Often, GMAT test takers find Problem Solving questions to be difficult, not because of their advanced math but because the questions involve equations that are either difficult to set up or difficult to work through (or both). At times, these questions almost seem to mock us with their relatively simplistic questions and ordinary answer choices. In these situations, Kaplan recommends using this to your advantage—because the question itself is clear and the answer choices themselves are simplistic, it is easier to work backward from these elements rather than to plow headfirst into the equation. This is what we call back-solving. Let's have a look at the three-step method for back-solving:

**Step 1: Estimate whether the answer will be small or large.**

**Step 2: Start with (B) or (D).**

**Step 3: If the answer you get is too big, try (B). If the answer you get is too small, try (D).**

By starting with **(B)** or **(D)**—as opposed to **(C)**—your chances of getting the correct answer double, because the answer choices are always listed in order from smallest to biggest. Therefore, if you start with **(C)**, there are three possibilities: **(C)** is right, **(C)** is too small, or **(C)** is too big. Only the first scenario produces a correct answer; the other two require more testing. It's the same with starting with **(A)** or **(E)**. If those aren't correct, you have a lot more testing to do!

If **(B)** is too small or **(D)** is too large, you'll have three choices left. In either case, testing the middle *remaining* choice immediately reveals the correct answer. For example, if you started with **(B)** and it was too small, you'd be left with **(C)**, **(D)**, or **(E)**. If **(D)** turns out to be too small, **(C)** is correct. If it's too large, **(E)** is correct. By following this system, you will never have to test more than two choices. In fact, you'll usually only have to test one.

Therefore, by starting with **(B)** or **(D)**, you have a two in five chance (40 percent likelihood) of locating the correct answer on your first try, compared to a 20 percent likelihood of success when you start with **(C)**. In addition, if you apply the "Do I think the answer will be small or big?" question first, you will greatly improve your chances of hitting the correct answer in one shot.

Let's try back-solving with our earlier example:

8. Employee *X* is paid $12.50 an hour no matter how many hours he works per week. Employee *Y* is paid $10 an hour for the first 30 hours she works in a week and 1.5 times that for each additional hour. On a certain week, both employees worked the same number of hours and were paid the same amount. How many hours did each employee work that week?

   ○ 48

   ○ 50

   ○ 54

   ○ 60

   ○ 64

**Step 1: Estimate whether the answer will be small or large.** Employee $Y$ gets the short end of the stick for a grueling 30 hours before things start looking up, so the two employees most likely worked for a large number of hours.

**Step 2: Start with (B) or (D).** Start by testing **(D)**:

Employee $X$ gets $12.50 \times 60 = \$750$ for 60 hours of work.

Employee $Y$ gets $10 \times 30 = \$300$ for the first 30 hours of work and ($10 \times 1.5$) $\times$ $(60 - 30) = \$15 \times 30 = \$450$ for the remaining 30 hours. That's a total paycheck of $300 + \$450 = \$750$.

Obviously, $750 = \$750$, so the two must have worked 60 hours each and we found that in one try! Had you started with **(B)**, you would've found it to be too small (Employee $X$, with his flat rate, would still be making more), and your next step would've been to test **(D)**.

Let's try some more examples.

9. Machine A can produce $\frac{1}{8}$ of a ton of nails in one hour. Machine B can produce $\frac{1}{12}$ of a ton of nails in one hour. Working together at their individual rates, how long would it take the two machines to produce one ton of nails?

   ◯ 4 hours
   ◯ 4 hours 48 minutes
   ◯ 5 hours
   ◯ 6 hours 20 minutes
   ◯ 10 hours

**Step 1: Estimate whether the answer will be small or large.** Machine B, the slower of the two, can produce of a $\frac{1}{12}$ ton of nails in one hour. If both machines were to work at this slower pace, they would produce $\frac{2}{12}$ of a ton of nails in one hour, and it would take them six hours to produce a ton. Because Machine A is quicker, the amount of time needed must be *shorter*.

**Step 2: Start with (B) or (D).** Start with (B):

Four hours and 48 minutes is $4\frac{4}{5} = \frac{24}{5}$ hours. In that time, Machine A would produce $\frac{1}{8} \times \frac{24}{5} = \frac{3}{5}$ of a ton, and Machine B would produce $\frac{1}{12} \times \frac{24}{5} = \frac{2}{5}$ of a ton for a total of $\frac{3}{5} + \frac{2}{5} = 1$ ton.

Choice **(B)** is correct, and there's no need to go further.

10. What is the value of $x$ if $\dfrac{x+1}{x-3} + \dfrac{x+2}{x-4} = 0$?

  ○ −2

  ○ −1

  ○ 0

  ○ 1

  ○ 2

**Step 1: Estimate whether the answer will be small or large.** It's incredibly difficult to estimate "small or big" with this one, but $x = 0$ is certainly easier to test than the others (simply cover up each $x$ with your fingers). Begin with **(C)**:

$$\frac{x+1}{x-3} + \frac{x+2}{x-4} = \frac{+1}{-3} - \frac{+2}{-4} = -\frac{1}{3} + \frac{2}{4} \neq 0$$

No need to add the resulting fractions as it's clear that they don't sum to 0.

**Step 2: Start with (B) or (D).** Therefore, **(C)** doesn't work. It's a bit difficult to tell whether 0 is too small or too large of a value for $x$, so proceed by testing **(D)**, the next easiest choice to test.

$$\frac{x+1}{x-3} + \frac{x+2}{x-4} = \frac{1+1}{1-3} - \frac{1+2}{1-4} = \frac{2}{-2} + \frac{3}{-3} = -1 - (-1) = -1 + 1 = 0$$

$x = 1$ gives us the desired result, making choice **(D)** correct.

Eager to give it a try? See how you do on these.

# PRACTICE SET

11. If $x$, $y$, and $z$ are positive numbers and $x - y = z$, then which of the following must equal 2?

$\bigcirc \quad \dfrac{x - y}{2z}$

$\bigcirc \quad \dfrac{x + y}{z + 2y}$

$\bigcirc \quad \dfrac{2y + 2z}{x + y}$

$\bigcirc \quad \dfrac{2x + 2y}{z + y}$

$\bigcirc \quad \dfrac{2x}{z + y}$

12. Stella buys a television set on an installment plan that requires her to pay $30 a month. If the total cost of the television is $270 and she has already paid off $120 of her debt, in how many months will she have completely paid off her debt?

$\bigcirc \quad 3$

$\bigcirc \quad 4$

$\bigcirc \quad 5$

$\bigcirc \quad 6$

$\bigcirc \quad 7$

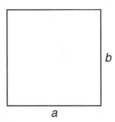

13. The diagram shown represents a square lawn. If $a$ is increased by 50 percent and $b$ is decreased by 20 percent, by what percent is the area of the lawn increased?

○ 15%

○ 20%

○ 30%

○ 45%

○ 70%

14. Carol lives 12 miles from the supermarket. She travels 3 miles from the supermarket to the post office, then 5 miles from the post office to the Laundromat. If the distance from Carol's house to the Laundromat is $p$ miles, which of the following represents the range of possible values for $p$?

○ $3 < p < 12$

○ $4 < p < 20$

○ $6 < p < 18$

○ $8 < p < 20$

○ $10 < p < 20$

15. If $\dfrac{n+5}{n-3} - \dfrac{n+3}{n-5} = 16$, then $n =$

○ -4

○ -2

○ 2

○ 4

○ 6

16. If $r$ and $s$ are both positive odd integers, which of the following must be true?

    ○ The sum of $r$ and $s$ is odd.

    ○ The product of $r$ and $s$ is even.

    ○ $r^s$ is odd.

    ○ $r - s$ is odd.

    ○ $r$ cannot be a multiple of $s$.

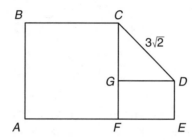

17. In the figure shown, the area of square $ABCF$ is 25, and $CDG$ is an isosceles right triangle. What is the area of rectangle $DEFG$?

    ○ 15

    ○ 12

    ○ 9

    ○ $6\sqrt{2}$

    ○ 6

18. A lawyer's representation costs $150 for the first hour and $125 for each additional hour. What is the total cost, in dollars, of her representation for $m$ hours, where $m$ is an integer greater than 1?

    ○ $150 + 125m$

    ○ $150 + 125(m - 1)$

    ○ $125 + 150m$

    ○ $125 + 150(m - 1)$

    ○ $275(m - 1)$

19. $\dfrac{1}{3^8} + \dfrac{1}{3^9} + \dfrac{1}{3^9} + \dfrac{1}{3^9} = ?$

- ○ $\dfrac{1}{3^6}$

- ○ $\dfrac{2}{3^8}$

- ○ $\dfrac{4}{3^8}$

- ○ $\dfrac{1}{3^{36}}$

- ○ $\dfrac{4}{3^{36}}$

20. A group of 30 tourists paid a total of $240 for admission to a museum exhibit. If the admission price for each adult was $10 and the admission price for each child was $5, how many adults were admitted to the exhibit?

- ○ 15
- ○ 18
- ○ 20
- ○ 22
- ○ 24

## THE WRAP-UP

GMAT Problem Solving questions are designed to *look* difficult and complex, but they don't have to be. While a basic understanding of mathematical concepts is needed, top scorers know that *what they know* math-wise isn't nearly as important as *how they use it*. Keep the following in mind:

- Picking numbers is great for problems with vague number references and no actual numbers.

- Back-solving works best when the question is clear, the choices are numbers, and the math is difficult to set up.

## ANSWERS AND EXPLANATIONS

### 11. (E)

With variables in the question stem and the answer choices, this problem is perfect for picking numbers. $x$, $y$, and $z$ are positive numbers such that $x - y = z$, so try $x = 3$, $y = 2$, and $z = 1$:

(A), $\dfrac{x-y}{2z} = \dfrac{3-2}{2(1)} = \dfrac{1}{2}$, so you can eliminate this.

(B), $\dfrac{x+y}{z+2y} = \dfrac{3+2}{1+2(2)} = \dfrac{5}{1+4} = \dfrac{5}{5} = 1$, so you can eliminate this.

(C), $\dfrac{2y+2z}{x+y} = \dfrac{2(2)+2(1)}{3+2} = \dfrac{4+2}{5} = \dfrac{6}{5}$, so you can eliminate this.

(D), $\dfrac{2x+y}{z+y} = \dfrac{2(3)+2}{1+2} = \dfrac{6+2}{3} = \dfrac{8}{3}$, so you can eliminate this.

(E), $\dfrac{2x}{z+y} = \dfrac{2(3)}{1+2} = \dfrac{6}{3} = 2$. Therefore, this works.

Because only **(E)** works, it must be the correct answer.

### 12. (C)

The television cost $270, $120 of which Stella already paid, so she still owes $270 − $120 = $150. At a repayment of $30 per month, $150 will take her $150 ÷ $30 per month = 5 months to repay. That's **(C)**.

### 13. (B)

Here you have a percent problem and no actual values, so pick 100 for $a$. Because the figure is a square, $a = b = 100$, and the original area is $100 \times 100 = 10,000$. Increasing $a$ by 50 percent changes its value to $100 + (50\%$ of $100) = 100 + 50 = 150$, and decreasing $b$ by 20 percent changes its value to $100 − (20\%$ of $100) = 100 − 20 = 80$, so the new area is $150 \times 80 = 12,000$. This is an increase of $12,000 − 10,000 = 2,000$ for a percent increase of $\dfrac{2,000}{10,000} = \dfrac{1}{5} = 20\%$. That's **(B)**.

**14. (B)**

There are two extremes in this scenario—one in which the Laundromat is as close to Carol's house as possible and one in which it's as far as possible—so it helps to draw a diagram for clarity. Because all five choices provide a different lower limit for $p$, identifying this lower limit will automatically net you the correct answer. The lower limit of $p$ occurs when the Laundromat is as close to Carol's house as possible, which puts it on a straight line between her house and the post office like so:

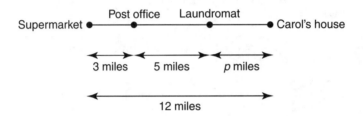

According to the diagram, the Laundromat could be as little as $12 - (3 + 5) = 12 - 8 = 4$ miles away from Carol's house. Only **(B)** begins with 4, so it must be correct.

**15. (D)**

An ugly algebra equation with numerical answer choices means back-solving is the way to go. Because the ugly mess on the left side of the equation comes out to 16, a fairly large whole number, let's start with choice **(D)**:

**(D)**, $\dfrac{n+5}{n-3} - \dfrac{n+3}{n-5} = \dfrac{4+5}{4-3} - \dfrac{4+3}{4-5} = \dfrac{9}{1} - \dfrac{7}{-1} = 9 + 7 = 16$. This works, so **(D)** is correct.

**16. (C)**

Problems that test number properties—such as those involving odd and even integers—are best handled with picking numbers. Because $r$ and $s$ are both positive odd integers, let's try $r = 1$ and $s = 3$:

**(A)**, $r + s = 1 + 3 = 4$, which is an even number, so eliminate this.

**(B)**, $r \times s = 1 \times 3 = 3$, which is an odd number, so eliminate this.

**(C)**, $r^s = 1^3 = 1$, which is an odd number, so hold on to this.

**(D)**, $r - s = 1 - 3 = -2$, which is an even number, so eliminate this.

**(E)**, 1 is not a multiple of 3, so keep this, too.

With two choices remaining, let's try $r = 3$ and $s = 1$:

**(C)**, $r^s = 3^1 = 3$, so keep this.

**(E)**, 3 is indeed a multiple of 1, so you can eliminate this.

Therefore, **(C)** must be correct.

### 17. (E)

With multiple figures, the key is to pass information from one figure to another. Square *ABCF* has an area of 25, so it must have a side of $\sqrt{25} = 5$. *CDG* is an isosceles right triangle with hypotenuse $3\sqrt{2}$, so its legs must each be 3. Putting all of that into the figure results in the following:

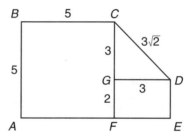

Therefore, the area of rectangle *DEFG* is $3 \times 2 = 6$. Choice **(E)** is correct.

### 18. (B)

With variables in the question stem and answer choices, picking numbers is the preferred method of attack. *m* must be greater than 1, so try *m* = 2. That puts the cost at $150 for the first hour and $125 for the additional hour for a total of $150 + $125 = $275. Plug 2 in for *m* into each of the five choices to see which comes out to $275:

**(A)**, 150 + 125(2) = 150 + 250 = 400, so you can eliminate this.

**(B)**, 150 + 125(2 − 1) = 150 + 125(1) = 275. Therefore, this works, and you can keep it.

**(C)**, 125 + 150(2) = 125 + 300 = 425, so eliminate this choice.

**(D)**, 125 + 150(2 − 1) = 125 + 150(1) = 275. Therefore, this also works, and you can keep it.

**(E)**, 275(2 − 1) = 275(1) = 275, and you can keep this because it works as well.

With three choices remaining, try another value for $m$, such as 3. Now the cost is $150 for the first hour and $125 for each additional hour for a total of $150 + $125(2) = $150 + $250 = $400:

**(B)**, 150 + 125(3 − 1) = 150 + 125(2) = 150 + 250 = 400. This still works, so keep it.

**(D)**, 125 + 150(3 − 1) = 125 + 150(2) = 125 + 300 = 425, so eliminate this.

**(E)**, 275(3 − 1) = 275(2) = 550, and you can eliminate this also.

Only **(B)** remains, so it must be correct.

### 19. (B)

To add a group of fractions, you must first find a common denominator. Because three of your fractions have a denominator of $3^9$, begin by converting the first fraction:

$$\frac{1}{3^8} \times \frac{3}{3} = \frac{3}{3^9}$$

Now add them:

$$\frac{3}{3^9} + \frac{1}{3^9} + \frac{1}{3^9} + \frac{1}{3^9} = \frac{6}{3^9} = \frac{3^1 \times 2}{3^9} = \frac{2}{3^8}$$

That matches **(B)**.

### 20. (B)

The question—how many adults were admitted—is fairly straightforward, but the equation can be a bit difficult to set up, so back-solve this one. Thirty tourists paid a total of $240, so the average price per ticket is $240 ÷ 30 = $8. This is pretty close to the average price for the two types of tickets, so start with a small choice.

Start with **(B)**: If the group of 30 tourists contained 18 adults, there would be 30 − 18 = 12 children. The adults would pay 18 × $10 = $180, and the children would pay 12 × $5 = $60 for a total price of $180 + $60 = $240. That fits the question, so this is the correct answer.

# CHAPTER 4: DATA SUFFICIENCY

While Problem Solving questions are quite similar to the math problems on other standardized tests, Data Sufficiency is unique to the GMAT. Similar to Problem Solving, Data Sufficiency questions primarily focus on high school-level arithmetic, algebra, and geometry. However, unlike Problem Solving, Data Sufficiency questions do not require you to *solve* the problem at hand—you only need to determine *if you have enough to solve it.* Many test takers are tempted to go all the way and solve—this is a *huge waste of time* that is better spent elsewhere.

Of the 37 questions in the Quantitative section, roughly 15 of them are of the Data Sufficiency variety, which accounts for about 40 percent of your Quantitative subscore.

While Data Sufficiency questions can take a little getting used to, a systematic approach will actually make them quicker and easier than Problem Solving questions. The directions for Data Sufficiency look something like this.

> **Directions:** Each question is followed by two statements, labeled (1) and (2), which contain certain data. Using these data, your knowledge of mathematics, and your familiarity with everyday facts (such as the number of minutes in an hour or the meaning of the word *clockwise*), decide whether the given data are sufficient to answer the question and then select the best choice from among the following:
>
> ○ Statement I ALONE is sufficient, but statement II alone is not sufficient to answer the question asked.
>
> ○ Statement II ALONE is sufficient, but statement I alone is not sufficient to answer the question asked.

○ BOTH statements I and II TOGETHER are sufficient to answer the
question asked, but NEITHER statement ALONE is sufficient to
answer the question asked.

○ EACH statement ALONE is sufficient to answer the question asked.

○ Statements I and II TOGETHER are NOT sufficient to answer
the question asked, and additional data specific to the problem
are needed.

**Notes:** In data sufficiency problems that ask for the value of a quantity,
the data given in the statements are sufficient only when it is possible to
determine exactly one numerical value for the quantity.

1. All numbers used are real numbers.

2. Figures conform to the information given in the question but
   might not conform to the additional information given in the two
   statements.

3. Lines shown are straight whether they appear straight or jagged.

4. Points, angles, regions, and so on exist in the order shown.

5. Angle measurements are positive.

6. All figures lie in a plane unless noted otherwise.

## THE DIRECTIONS

The most important thing to note here is that you're *not* looking for any numerical
values. The only thing you are interested in is whether you *could find* such a value
with the information given. The only unit conversions you need to know are those
involving time. You will be given any conversions for lengths, weights, etc. that
you need.

## THE ANSWER CHOICES

In Data Sufficiency, the choices never change. Memorizing them now means not
having to read them on Test Day when the clock is ticking.

## THE NOTES

The notes are here to make your life easier by closing up "what if" loopholes. *Sufficient* means only **one** possible result, numbers aren't imaginary, figures consist of straight lines, and things are as they appear unless otherwise noted.

## THE STRATEGY

Because the choices never change, Kaplan advises that you memorize them for Test Day. If you've ever played hopscotch as a kid, you might remember cheaters going, "1, 2, 10!" If so, be sure to thank that cheater, because the mnemonic 1-2-TEN is an easy way to remember the order of the five choices:

- **1** ALONE is sufficient.

- **2** ALONE is sufficient.

- **T**ogether the statements are sufficient.

- **E**ither statement is sufficient.

- **N**either statement is sufficient (not even together).

Also, it'll help to redraw figures to conform to the data in the statements. For example, if statement I says *AB* = 2*AC*, the triangle on the left would need to be redrawn to look like the one on the right:

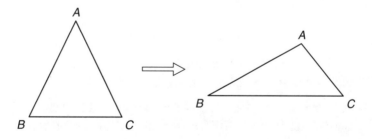

# THE METHOD

The most difficult part of a Data Sufficiency question is having an efficient way to work through the choices. For some, wrong choices are chosen simply due to the confusion behind what *sufficient* means and how properly to test for it. The best way to avoid such confusion is to have a clear, systematic way of evaluating the choices in the least amount of time.

## KAPLAN'S 3-STEP METHOD FOR DATA SUFFICIENCY QUESTIONS

**Step 1: Focus on the question stem.**

**Step 2: Evaluate each statement separately, eliminating wrong choices as you do.**

**Step 3: Evaluate the statements together *only if* they are individually insufficient.**

Let's apply this method to the following example.

1. Team *X* won 40 basketball games. What percent of its basketball games did team *X* win?

   I.   Team *X* played the same number of games as team *Y*.
   II.  Team *Y* won 24 games, which is 50 percent of the games it played.

   ○ Statement I ALONE is sufficient, but statement II alone is not sufficient to answer the question asked.

   ○ Statement II ALONE is sufficient, but statement I alone is not sufficient to answer the question asked.

   ○ BOTH statements I and II TOGETHER are sufficient to answer the question asked, but NEITHER statement ALONE is sufficient to answer the question asked.

   ○ EACH statement ALONE is sufficient to answer the question asked.

   ○ Statements I and II TOGETHER are NOT sufficient to answer the question asked, and additional data specific to the problem are needed.

**Step 1: Focus on the question stem.**

> 1. Team $X$ won 40 basketball games. What percent of its basketball games did team $X$ win?

We're looking for the percent of its games that team $X$ won. Figuring out a percent requires the part and the whole. The question stem gives us the part, so a statement is sufficient if it can provide us **one and only one** value for the total number of games played by team $X$.

**Step 2: Evaluate each statement separately, eliminating wrong choices as you do.**
Focus on each statement separately. Start with statement I:

> I. Team $X$ played the same number of games as team $Y$.

Without our knowing how many games team $Y$ played, this statement does not help. Statement I is not sufficient, so eliminate choices **(A)** and **(D)**.

Now concentrate on statement II by itself:

> II. Team $Y$ won 24 games, which is 50 percent of the games it played.

Whether or not you knew that 24 is 50 percent of 48 is not important. What *is* important is that 24 is 50 percent of **one and only one** number. Statement II allows us to figure out the total number of games team $Y$ played. Be careful, as this is where a lot of test takers fall into the test maker's trap. It is important that you do not accidentally incorporate statement I's information when evaluating statement II alone. Statement II is not sufficient, so eliminate choice **(B)**.

**Step 3: Evaluate the statements together *only if* they are individually insufficient.**
Now let's consider both statements together:

> I. Team $X$ played the same number of games as team $Y$.
> II. Team $Y$ won 24 games, which is 50 percent of the games it played.

Statement II gave us one unique value for the number of games played by team $Y$. Statement I tells us that the two teams played the same number of games. Putting this information together, we have **one and only one** value for the number of games played by team $X$. The statements taken together are sufficient, so **(C)** is correct.

Let's try some more.

2. If $2b - 2a^2 = 18$, what is the value of $b$?

    I.  $a^2 = 1{,}156$
    II.  $a > 0$

- ⬭ Statement I ALONE is sufficient, but statement II alone is not sufficient to answer the question asked.
- ⬭ Statement II ALONE is sufficient, but statement I alone is not sufficient to answer the question asked.
- ⬭ BOTH statements I and II TOGETHER are sufficient to answer the question asked, but NEITHER statement ALONE is sufficient to answer the question asked.
- ⬭ EACH statement ALONE is sufficient to answer the question asked.
- ⬭ Statements I and II TOGETHER are NOT sufficient to answer the question asked, and additional data specific to the problem are needed.

**Step 1: Focus on the question stem.**

2. If $2b - 2a^2 = 18$, what is the value of $b$?

The equation has two variables, so a statement will only be sufficient if it gives you a unique value for one of them.

**Step 2: Evaluate each statement separately, eliminating wrong choices as you do.**
Begin with statement I:

    I.  $a^2 = 1{,}156$

While $a$ can have two values (positive and negative), $a^2$ only has one. Statement I allows us to evaluate $2a^2$, and the equation becomes $2b - 2(1{,}156) = 18$. On Test Day, it is extremely important that you do not waste time solving for $b$ here. You only need to know that you *can* solve for $b$ at this point. Statement I is sufficient, so eliminate choices **(B)**, **(C)**, and **(E)**.

Now let's look at statement II by itself:

II. $a > 0$

Statement II provides us with infinitely many possible values for $a$. Statement II is not sufficient, so (**A**) is correct.

**Step 3: Evaluate the statements together *only if* they are individually insufficient.**
We do not need to do step 3 in this case.

3. Jack and Dianne are in line to purchase movie tickets. There are 32 people in front of Jack and 40 people behind Dianne. How many people are there in the line?

   I. There are 13 people between Jack and Dianne.
   II. There are fewer people in front of Jack than there are in front of Dianne.

   ○ Statement I ALONE is sufficient, but statement II alone is not sufficient to answer the question asked.

   ○ Statement II ALONE is sufficient, but statement I alone is not sufficient to answer the question asked.

   ○ BOTH statements I and II TOGETHER are sufficient to answer the question asked, but NEITHER statement ALONE is sufficient to answer the question asked.

   ○ EACH statement ALONE is sufficient to answer the question asked.

   ○ Statements I and II TOGETHER are NOT sufficient to answer the question asked, and additional data specific to the problem are needed.

**Step 1: Focus on the question stem.**

3. Jack and Dianne are in line to purchase movie tickets. There are 32 people in front of Jack and 40 people behind Dianne. How many people are there in the line?

The question can be a bit confusing, so it may help to sketch the different ways that the lines could be arranged. You might draw something like this:

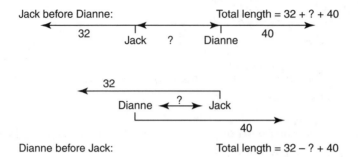

According to the diagram, we'll need two pieces of information to determine the length of the line:

1. Is Jack in front of Dianne or is Dianne in front of Jack?

2. How many people are between Jack and Dianne?

**Step 2: Evaluate each statement separately, eliminating wrong choices as you do.**
Begin with statement I:

    I.  There are 13 people between Jack and Dianne.

This gives you half of the information needed. Without knowing if Jack is in front of or behind Dianne, you cannot determine the length of the line. Statement I is not sufficient, so eliminate **(A)** and **(D)**.

Now look at statement II by itself:

    II.  There are fewer people in front of Jack than there are in front of Dianne.

This tells you that Jack is in front of Dianne. However, with this statement alone, we do not know how many people are between the two of them. (Remember not to lump statement I's information here!) Statement II is not sufficient, so eliminate **(B)**.

**Step 3: Evaluate the statements together *only if* they are individually insufficient.**
Now consider both statements together:

    I.  There are 13 people between Jack and Dianne.
    II.  There are fewer people in front of Jack than there are in front of Dianne.

Taking the statements together, we know the number of people between the two, and we know that Jack is in front of Dianne. This answers both of the questions we had in step 1. The statements taken together are sufficient, so **(C)** is correct.

4. Is $x > y$?

      I.  $x > z + 1$
      II.  $y > z$

    ◯ Statement I ALONE is sufficient, but statement II alone is not sufficient to answer the question asked.

    ◯ Statement II ALONE is sufficient, but statement I alone is not sufficient to answer the question asked.

    ◯ BOTH statements I and II TOGETHER are sufficient to answer the question asked, but NEITHER statement ALONE is sufficient to answer the question asked.

    ◯ EACH statement ALONE is sufficient to answer the question asked.

    ◯ Statements I and II TOGETHER are NOT sufficient to answer the question asked, and additional data specific to the problem are needed.

**Step 1: Focus on the question stem.**

4. Is $x > y$?

Some Data Sufficiency problems, such as this one, pose a yes/no question rather than asking for a numerical value. In these questions, note that both a "definite yes" or "definite no" is considered sufficient. The only way for a statement to not be sufficient is if the result is "sometimes yes/sometimes no." In this question, we will need at least the relative values of $x$ and $y$ to determine sufficiency.

**Step 2: Evaluate each statement separately, eliminating wrong choices as you do.**
Begin with statement I:

      I.  $x > z + 1$

Statement I tells you nothing about the relationship between $x$ and $y$. Statement I is not sufficient, so eliminate **(A)** and **(D)**.

Now look at statement II by itself:

    II. $y > z$

Statement II also tells you nothing about the relationship between $x$ and $y$. Statement II is not sufficient, so eliminate **(B)**.

**Step 3: Evaluate the statements together *only if* they are individually insufficient.** Now consider both statements together:

    I. $x > z + 1$
    II. $y > z$

Taken together, the statements still do not give you the relationship between $x$ and $y$. While you know that both are greater than $z$, there is no way to tell how much greater than $z$ each is. For example, $y$ being greater than $z$ does not prevent it from being greater than $z + 1$, $z + 2$, $z + 3$, and so on. The statements taken together are not sufficient, so **(E)** is correct.

    5. Is $x > 1$?

        I. $x^2 < x$
        II. $x$ is positive.

    ◯ Statement I ALONE is sufficient, but statement II alone is not sufficient to answer the question asked.

    ◯ Statement II ALONE is sufficient, but statement I alone is not sufficient to answer the question asked.

    ◯ BOTH statements I and II TOGETHER are sufficient to answer the question asked, but NEITHER statement ALONE is sufficient to answer the question asked.

    ◯ EACH statement ALONE is sufficient to answer the question asked.

    ◯ Statements I and II TOGETHER are NOT sufficient to answer the question asked, and additional data specific to the problem are needed.

**Step 1: Focus on the question stem.**

> 5. Is $x > 1$?

We'll need the value of $x$ (or a narrow enough range of values) to answer this yes/no question.

**Step 2: Evaluate each statement separately, eliminating wrong choices as you do.** Begin with statement I:

> I. $x^2 < x$

The only way for statement I to be true is if $x$ is a fraction between 0 and 1, as these are the only numbers that get smaller when you square them. Statement I is sufficient to answer "no" to the question, so eliminate **(B)**, **(C)**, and **(E)**.

Now look at statement II by itself:

> II. $x$ is positive.

Statement II doesn't help you here. A positive value of $x$ *could* be less than 1 (such as $x = 0.5$) or greater than 1, so there isn't enough information to answer this question either way. Statement II is not sufficient, so **(A)** is correct.

**Step 3: Evaluate the statements together *only if* they are individually insufficient.** There is no need to do step 3 in this case.

**Remember:** A "no" answer is sufficient, but "no answer" is not!

Think you've got it? Try your hand at the following practice problems to find out!

## PRACTICE SET

6. What is the value of $x$?

   I. $x$ is 50% of 4.
   II. $x$ is the average (arithmetic mean) of 0, 1, and 5.

   ○ Statement I ALONE is sufficient, but statement II alone is not sufficient to answer the question asked.

   ○ Statement II ALONE is sufficient, but statement I alone is not sufficient to answer the question asked.

   ○ BOTH statements I and II TOGETHER are sufficient to answer the question asked, but NEITHER statement ALONE is sufficient to answer the question asked.

   ○ EACH statement ALONE is sufficient to answer the question asked.

   ○ Statements I and II TOGETHER are NOT sufficient to answer the question asked, and additional data specific to the problem are needed.

7. What is the value of $x$?

   I. $x$ is positive.
   II. $x^3 = 8$

   ○ Statement I ALONE is sufficient, but statement II alone is not sufficient to answer the question asked.

   ○ Statement II ALONE is sufficient, but statement I alone is not sufficient to answer the question asked.

   ○ BOTH statements I and II TOGETHER are sufficient to answer the question asked, but NEITHER statement ALONE is sufficient to answer the question asked.

   ○ EACH statement ALONE is sufficient to answer the question asked.

   ○ Statements I and II TOGETHER are NOT sufficient to answer the question asked, and additional data specific to the problem are needed.

8. What is the value of $x$?

    I. $x + 5 = 7$
    II. $x$ is less than 3.

    ○ Statement I ALONE is sufficient, but statement II alone is not sufficient to answer the question asked.

    ○ Statement II ALONE is sufficient, but statement I alone is not sufficient to answer the question asked.

    ○ BOTH statements I and II TOGETHER are sufficient to answer the question asked, but NEITHER statement ALONE is sufficient to answer the question asked.

    ○ EACH statement ALONE is sufficient to answer the question asked.

    ○ Statements I and II TOGETHER are NOT sufficient to answer the question asked, and additional data specific to the problem are needed.

9. What is the value of $x$?

    I. $x$ is an integer less than 2.
    II. $x$ is an integer greater than 0.

    ○ Statement I ALONE is sufficient, but statement II alone is not sufficient to answer the question asked.

    ○ Statement II ALONE is sufficient, but statement I alone is not sufficient to answer the question asked.

    ○ BOTH statements I and II TOGETHER are sufficient to answer the question asked, but NEITHER statement ALONE is sufficient to answer the question asked.

    ○ EACH statement ALONE is sufficient to answer the question asked.

    ○ Statements I and II TOGETHER are NOT sufficient to answer the question asked, and additional data specific to the problem are needed.

10. Paul's taxes were what percent of his salary?

    I.  Paul's salary was $25,000.
    II. Paul's year-end bonus was 5 percent of his salary.

    ○ Statement I ALONE is sufficient, but statement II alone is not sufficient to answer the question asked.

    ○ Statement II ALONE is sufficient, but statement I alone is not sufficient to answer the question asked.

    ○ BOTH statements I and II TOGETHER are sufficient to answer the question asked, but NEITHER statement ALONE is sufficient to answer the question asked.

    ○ EACH statement ALONE is sufficient to answer the question asked.

    ○ Statements I and II TOGETHER are NOT sufficient to answer the question asked, and additional data specific to the problem are needed.

11. What is the value of $x$?

    I.  $\dfrac{x}{20} = 0.425$

    II. $\dfrac{x-4}{2} = 2.25$

    ○ Statement I ALONE is sufficient, but statement II alone is not sufficient to answer the question asked.

    ○ Statement II ALONE is sufficient, but statement I alone is not sufficient to answer the question asked.

    ○ BOTH statements I and II TOGETHER are sufficient to answer the question asked, but NEITHER statement ALONE is sufficient to answer the question asked.

    ○ EACH statement ALONE is sufficient to answer the question asked.

    ○ Statements I and II TOGETHER are NOT sufficient to answer the question asked, and additional data specific to the problem are needed.

12. Is $\dfrac{n}{3} = \dfrac{8}{12}$ ?

    I.  $n > 1$
    II.  $n < 3$

- ◯ Statement I ALONE is sufficient, but statement II alone is not sufficient to answer the question asked.

- ◯ Statement II ALONE is sufficient, but statement I alone is not sufficient to answer the question asked.

- ◯ BOTH statements I and II TOGETHER are sufficient to answer the question asked, but NEITHER statement ALONE is sufficient to answer the question asked.

- ◯ EACH statement ALONE is sufficient to answer the question asked.

- ◯ Statements I and II TOGETHER are NOT sufficient to answer the question asked, and additional data specific to the problem are needed.

13. Did Mr. Moss's savings account increase by more than 40 percent from 1981 to 1989?

    I.  Mr. Moss's savings account in 1989 was 1.52 times his savings account in 1981.
    II.  Mr. Moss's savings account in 1989 was $380,000.

- ◯ Statement I ALONE is sufficient, but statement II alone is not sufficient to answer the question asked.

- ◯ Statement II ALONE is sufficient, but statement I alone is not sufficient to answer the question asked.

- ◯ BOTH statements I and II TOGETHER are sufficient to answer the question asked, but NEITHER statement ALONE is sufficient to answer the question asked.

- ◯ EACH statement ALONE is sufficient to answer the question asked.

- ◯ Statements I and II TOGETHER are NOT sufficient to answer the question asked, and additional data specific to the problem are needed.

14. What is the ratio of men to women at the benefit luncheon?

   I. There were 30 women at the benefit luncheon.
   II. At the benefit luncheon, the number of men was 50 percent less than the number of women.

   ⬭ Statement I ALONE is sufficient, but statement II alone is not sufficient to answer the question asked.

   ⬭ Statement II ALONE is sufficient, but statement I alone is not sufficient to answer the question asked.

   ⬭ BOTH statements I and II TOGETHER are sufficient to answer the question asked, but NEITHER statement ALONE is sufficient to answer the question asked.

   ⬭ EACH statement ALONE is sufficient to answer the question asked.

   ⬭ Statements I and II TOGETHER are NOT sufficient to answer the question asked, and additional data specific to the problem are needed.

15. Is $|x - y| = 1$?

   I. $x$ and $y$ are consecutive integers.
   II. $x$ is even and $y$ is odd.

   ⬭ Statement I ALONE is sufficient, but statement II alone is not sufficient to answer the question asked.

   ⬭ Statement II ALONE is sufficient, but statement I alone is not sufficient to answer the question asked.

   ⬭ BOTH statements I and II TOGETHER are sufficient to answer the question asked, but NEITHER statement ALONE is sufficient to answer the question asked.

   ⬭ EACH statement ALONE is sufficient to answer the question asked.

   ⬭ Statements I and II TOGETHER are NOT sufficient to answer the question asked, and additional data specific to the problem are needed.

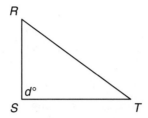

16. In the figure shown, if $ST = 6$ and $RT = 8$, what is the length of segment $RS$?

    I.  $\triangle RST$ has a perimeter of 24.

    II.  $d = 90$

◯ Statement I ALONE is sufficient, but statement II alone is not sufficient to answer the question asked.

◯ Statement II ALONE is sufficient, but statement I alone is not sufficient to answer the question asked.

◯ BOTH statements I and II TOGETHER are sufficient to answer the question asked, but NEITHER statement ALONE is sufficient to answer the question asked.

◯ EACH statement ALONE is sufficient to answer the question asked.

◯ Statements I and II TOGETHER are NOT sufficient to answer the question asked, and additional data specific to the problem are needed.

17. A rectangular floor 10 meters long is to be entirely covered with nonoverlapping square tiles, each with a side of length 0.5 meters with no portion of tile left over. What is the least number of such tiles that will be necessary to complete the job?

    I. The area of the floor is 25 square meters.
    II. The width of the floor is $\frac{1}{4}$ of the length.

    ◯ Statement I ALONE is sufficient, but statement II alone is not sufficient to answer the question asked.

    ◯ Statement II ALONE is sufficient, but statement I alone is not sufficient to answer the question asked.

    ◯ BOTH statements I and II TOGETHER are sufficient to answer the question asked, but NEITHER statement ALONE is sufficient to answer the question asked.

    ◯ EACH statement ALONE is sufficient to answer the question asked.

    ◯ Statements I and II TOGETHER are NOT sufficient to answer the question asked, and additional data specific to the problem are needed.

18. Benny, a real estate agent, receives a commission of 8 percent of the selling price for every house he sells. What was the selling price of the house he sold most recently?

    I. The selling price was 300 percent greater than the original purchase price.
    II. The selling price minus Benny's commission was $176,000.

    ◯ Statement I ALONE is sufficient, but statement II alone is not sufficient to answer the question asked.

    ◯ Statement II ALONE is sufficient, but statement I alone is not sufficient to answer the question asked.

    ◯ BOTH statements I and II TOGETHER are sufficient to answer the question asked, but NEITHER statement ALONE is sufficient to answer the question asked.

    ◯ EACH statement ALONE is sufficient to answer the question asked.

    ◯ Statements I and II TOGETHER are NOT sufficient to answer the question asked, and additional data specific to the problem are needed.

19. If 25 percent of the surface area of right circular cylinder $X$ is shaded and 40 percent of the surface area of right circular cylinder $Y$ is shaded, what is the area of the shaded portion of right circular cylinder $X$?

    I. The area of the shaded portion of the surface area of cylinder $X$ is 75 percent of the area of the shaded portion of the surface area of cylinder $Y$.

    II. The surface area of cylinder $Y$ is 10.

   ◯  Statement I ALONE is sufficient, but statement II alone is not sufficient to answer the question asked.

   ◯  Statement II ALONE is sufficient, but statement I alone is not sufficient to answer the question asked.

   ◯  BOTH statements I and II TOGETHER are sufficient to answer the question asked, but NEITHER statement ALONE is sufficient to answer the question asked.

   ◯  EACH statement ALONE is sufficient to answer the question asked.

   ◯  Statements I and II TOGETHER are NOT sufficient to answer the question asked, and additional data specific to the problem are needed.

# THE WRAP-UP

Data Sufficiency can be quite manageable (and even enjoyable!) if approached in a focused, systematic way. It's important to remember that you should *never* be in the habit of solving outright—you should *only* do as much as necessary to determine if you *can* solve. Keep the following in mind:

- Data Sufficiency choices never change, so memorize them with **1-2-TEN**.

- For Data Sufficiency questions that want a value, *sufficient* means **only one possible value.**

- For yes/no Data Sufficiency questions, *sufficient* is **either "definite yes" or "definite no."**

# ANSWERS AND EXPLANATIONS

### 6. (D)

Whether or not you can quickly tell that statement I evaluates to 2 is unimportant. The only thing you need to know is that "50% of 4" can only have one unique result. Statement I is sufficient, so eliminate choices **(B)**, **(C)**, and **(E)**.

Statement II might take a bit longer to evaluate but once again, it is important that you get in the habit of *not* doing so. For any list of known numbers, there can only be one average. Because the two statements will never conflict, that average must also be 2. Statement II is also sufficient, so **(D)** is correct.

### 7. (B)

With statement I, $x$ can be any number from an infinite list of positive integers. Statement I is not sufficient, so eliminate **(A)** and **(D)**.

Statement II provides much more to work with. Once again, it isn't important whether or not you know that the cube root of 8 is 2. What is important to know is that even roots can have two possible values (positive and negative), while odd roots can only have one. Statement II is sufficient, and **(B)** is correct.

### 8. (A)

The equation in statement I evaluates to one and only one value for $x$ (2 in this case.) Statement I is sufficient, so eliminate **(B)**, **(C)**, and **(E)**.

Statement II provides plenty of options for the value of $x$. How many options isn't important—you only need to know that it's more than one. Statement II is not sufficient, so **(A)** is correct.

### 9. (C)

Statement I says $x$ is an integer and less than 2. That does not narrow it down to one specific value. Statement I is not sufficient, so eliminate **(A)** and **(D)**.

Statement II says $x$ is an integer and greater than 0. That does not narrow it down either. Statement II is not sufficient, so eliminate **(B)**.

Only one integer is both less than 2 and greater than 0. The statements taken together are sufficient, so **(C)** is correct.

**10. (E)**

To answer the question, you need to know Paul's salary and the amount he paid in taxes or some kind of relationship between the two.

Statement I provides Paul's salary but tells you nothing about the taxes. Statement II is not sufficient, so eliminate **(A)** and **(D)**.

Statement II does not help. The year-end bonus is completely irrelevant, so this information is useless.

Combining the statements still leaves us with no information about Paul's taxes. The statements taken together are not sufficient, so **(E)** is correct.

**11. (D)**

In statement I, cross multiplying (don't waste time doing it!) gives you the value of $x$. Statement I is sufficient, so eliminate **(B)**, **(C)**, and **(E)**.

Cross multiplying statement II also allows you to solve for $x$. Statement II is also sufficient, so **(D)** is correct.

**12. (E)**

The given equation is only true if $n = 2$, because $\dfrac{8}{12} = \dfrac{2}{3}$, so the question is really asking if $n = 2$.

Statement I tells you that $n > 1$, but an infinite number of possibilities can satisfy this requirement. Statement I is not sufficient, so eliminate **(A)** and **(D)**.

Statement II tells you that $n < 3$, but that produces just as many possible values as does statement I's information. Statement II is not sufficient, so eliminate **(B)**.

While you might believe that the two statements taken together would force $n$ to be 2, it is not the case, as neither statement requires $n$ to be an integer. $n$ could be 2, but it could also be 1.5, 2.3, and so on. The statements taken together are not sufficient, so **(E)** is correct.

**13. (A)**

To answer this question, you either need Mr. Moss's actual savings amounts from both 1981 and 1989 or a relationship between those two amounts.

Statement I says that his 1989 amount is 1.52 times that of his 1981 amount. This is the same as saying that he had 152 percent of his 1981 amount in 1989, which translates into a 52 percent increase. Statement I is sufficient, so eliminate **(B)**, **(C)**, and **(E)**.

Statement II provides his 1989 amount and says nothing about his 1981 total. Statement II is not sufficient, so **(A)** is correct.

**14. (B)**

To find the ratio, you need either the actual number of men and women at the luncheon or a relationship between the two that can be restated as a ratio.

Statement I tells you the number of women but does not provide any information about the men. Statement I is not sufficient, so eliminate **(A)** and **(E)**.

Statement II tells you that the number of men was 50 percent less than the number of women, which can be restated as a ratio. Statement II is sufficient, so **(B)** is correct.

**15. (A)**

To answer this question, you need either the actual values of $x$ and $y$ or their relationship.

Statement I says they are consecutive, so either $x + 1 = y$ or $y + 1 = x$. That means $x - y$ is either 1 or −1. Therefore, $|x - y|$ must be 1. Statement I is sufficient, so eliminate **(B)**, **(C)**, and **(E)**.

Statement II does not help, as knowing that $x$ is even and $y$ is odd tells you nothing about their relative values. Statement II is not sufficient, so **(A)** is correct.

**16. (D)**

To find the length of $RS$, you need information about $\triangle RST$ that expresses the relationship among the side lengths.

With the perimeter in statement I, you can determine the length of the third side by subtracting the two provided in the question. Statement I is sufficient, so eliminate **(B)**, **(C)**, and **(E)**.

Statement II makes $\Delta RST$ a right triangle, which allows you to use the Pythagorean theorem to find the length of $RS$. Statement II is also sufficient, so **(D)** is correct.

### 17. (D)

The area of a rectangle is length × width. The tiles are squares, so their area is side$^2$. The question provides the side of the tile and the length of the floor, so the only thing you need is the floor's width.

Statement I gives you the area of the floor. Because have the length, you can figure out the width. Statement I is sufficient, so eliminate **(B)**, **(C)**, and **(E)**.

Statement II tells you the relationship between the width and the length, which would also allow you to figure out the width. Statement II is also sufficient, so **(D)** is correct.

### 18. (B)

You know the commission is 8 percent of the sales price, so to find that price, you need the amount of the commission.

The original purchase price is completely irrelevant, so statement I tells you nothing. Statement I is not sufficient, so eliminate **(A)** and **(D)**.

Statement II provides the difference between the sales price and the commission. Because the commission is 8 percent of the sales price, this is enough information to solve the problem (sales price − 8% of sales price = $176,000, so $176,000 is 92% of the sales price). Statement II is sufficient, so **(B)** is correct.

### 19. (C)

Don't let the cylinders scare you. You don't need to know anything about them to answer this question! You are given each cylinder's shaded percentage, but you don't have their actual surface areas, so look for that in the statements.

Statement I gives you the relationship between the areas of the shaded portions for $X$ and $Y$. However, without the actual surface area of either cylinder, you cannot answer the question. Statement I is not sufficient, so eliminate **(A)** and **(D)**.

Statement II gives you the surface area of $Y$, but that tells you nothing about $X$. Statement II is not sufficient, so eliminate **(B)**.

Combining the two statements, you have the surface area of $Y$ and the relationship between $Y$ and $X$, which is enough to figure out the surface area of $X$ and answer the question. The statements taken together are sufficient, so **(C)** is correct.

# CHAPTER 5: **SENTENCE CORRECTION**

Sentence Correction questions test your ability to choose the best version of a sentence out of five responses based on the rules of standard written English. While there are, alas, many rules of standard written English, the GMAT most commonly concentrates on the following five:

- **Verb usage** (proper agreement and correct tense)
- **Reference** (proper use of pronouns and modifiers)
- **Parallel structure** (consistency among items in a list or comparison)
- **Idioms** (proper use of idiomatic expressions)
- **Style** (avoiding excess verbiage, using active verbs, etc.)

Of the 41 questions in the Verbal section, you can expect around 16 of them to be Sentence Correction, which accounts for 40 percent of your Verbal subscore.

Developing a method for attacking Sentence Correction questions and reviewing the common Sentence Correction errors will help you maximize your performance on this question type. The directions for Sentence Correction look something like this:

> **Directions:** Each question presents a sentence, part or all of which is underlined. Beneath the sentence, you will find five ways of phrasing the underlined part. The first repeats the original while the other four are different. Choose the best answer according to the rules of standard written English, paying attention to grammar, word choice, and sentence construction. Select the answer that produces the most effective sentence—the resulting sentence should be clear, exact, and free of grammatical error. It should also minimize awkwardness, ambiguity, and redundancy.

The directions are rather long, so get to know them now to avoid having to read them on Test Day while the clock is running. Basically, you are looking for the best choice, which the GMAT defines as "clear, exact, and free of grammatical error." The test makers also want something that isn't awkward, ambiguous, or redundant.

As noted in the directions, Sentence Correction problems will present a sentence with either part or all of it underlined. The first choice will always be identical to the underlined portion, so you should *never* waste time reading it.

# THE STRATEGY

Because the vast majority of Sentence Correction errors violate one of the five rules listed earlier, the best way to master this question type is by knowing these rules. Let's practice each in turn.

## VERB USAGE

GMAT test makers know that most people have no trouble with subject-verb agreement, so they try to confuse the issue by putting as much space between a verb and its subject as possible.

**Rule:** A verb must agree with its subject in number and type, and its tense must fit the rest of the sentence.

### Strategy Exercise 1

*Choose the verb that agrees with the subject.*

A. Each of the entertainers involved in the festivities (was / were) paid in advance.

B. A series of sightings of UFOs (has / have) turned the town into a tourist mecca.

C. There (is / are) a number of delicious ways to prepare artichokes.

D. The convict escaped from custody and is thought (to flee / to have fled) the country.

E. I (did not see / do not seen / have not seen) him since last Saturday.

F. She had shut the door when she realized that she (won't be / wouldn't be) able to reopen it.

## Answers and Explanations

A. **was**

The prepositional phrases containing plurals that follow the subject are there to confuse you. *Each* is singular, so it must be followed by a singular verb.

B. **has**

The subject is *series,* which is always singular. Watch out for singular subjects like *series, string, spate,* and *succession,* as they are often followed by prepositional phrases containing plurals.

C. **are**

In "There is" and "There are" sentences, the subject follows the verb. Here, "a number of" (meaning *several*) indicates a plural subject (as it always will on the GMAT).

D. **to have fled**

The convict has already escaped, so the logical belief is that he has already fled the country.

E. **have not seen**

The *since* in the sentence tells you that the (non)activity under discussion began in the past and continues into the present, so you should use the present perfect tense.

F. **wouldn't be**

When the verb in question refers to the future as contemplated in the past, you should use the past tense of *will,* or *would,* as in "wouldn't be."

# REFERENCE

There are two rules of reference:

**Rule:** A pronoun must unambiguously refer to one antecedent, agreeing in both number and type.

**Rule:** A modifier must unambiguously refer to one appropriate antecedent.

Therefore:

1. Whenever you see a pronoun underlined, immediately check its antecedent (the noun it is replacing).

2. Modifier errors can be tough to spot because they don't always "sound wrong."

## Strategy Exercise 2

*Choose the correct pronoun.*

A. The company had promised to diversify, but (it / they) later reneged on the agreement.

B. If the partners can't resolve their differences, the courts may have to do (it / so).

### Answers and Explanations

A. **it**

Watch out for collective nouns like *company*, *committee*, *group*, and *gang*, which require singular pronouns.

B. **so**

*It* makes no sense here, as there is no antecedent noun for *it* to refer to.

## Strategy Exercise 3

*Choose the correct modifier.*

A. While eating spaghetti, (a meatball rolled / I let a meatball roll).

B. He laid the trousers (flat / flatly) upon the table.

### Answers and Explanations

A. **I let a meatball roll**

Unless the meatball was in fact eating spaghetti as it rolled off the plate, it should be assumed that the subject of the modifying phrase "While eating spaghetti" is *I*.

B. **flat**

The modifier here refers to the trousers, so the adjective form *flat* is correct.

## PARALLEL STRUCTURE

Whenever a sentence contains either a comparison or list, check for parallel structure issues.

**Rule:** Items in either a comparison or a list must all be in the same grammatical form.

### Strategy Exercise 4

*Choose the phrase that fits the sentence.*

A. I remember my aunt making her own dandelion wine and (playing the fiddle / that she played the fiddle).

B. To visualize success is not the same as (to achieve / achieving) it.

C. The article questioned the popularity of jazz compared to (that of popular music / popular music).

D. The challenger weighed 20 pounds less than (that of the defender / the defender).

### Answers and Explanations

A. **playing the fiddle**
   My aunt is "making" her wine, so to parallel that, she needs to be "playing" the fiddle.

B. **to achieve**
   The infinitive form "to visualize" must parallel another infinitive, so "to achieve" is correct.

C. **that of popular music**
   "The popularity of jazz" needs to be compared to the popularity of music, not the music itself.

D. **the defender**
   People are being compared, so this is correct.

## IDIOMS

As anyone who's ever studied a foreign language can tell you, learning proper idioms can be extremely difficult because there is no general rule, only lists to memorize. When it comes to GMAT English, either your ear will recognize the correct idiom, or you should take the time to learn the idioms you don't know.

**Rule:** There isn't one!

### Strategy Exercise 5

*Correctly complete the idiom.*

A. Mathew Brady is regarded (as / to be) one of America's greatest photographers.

B. The destruction of the ozone is (considered / considered as) a major health threat.

C. It took us twice as long to do it together (as / than) it would have taken me by myself.

D. Her client didn't tell her (if / whether) he had sent his payment yet.

E. Jewel is not only a great singer (but / but also / but also is) a talented poetess.

F. I (either must read / must either read / must read either) the newspaper or listen to the radio before I go to work.

### Answers and Explanations

**Note:** The right answers in this section are simply right because they are correct idiomatic usage.

A. **as**

B. **considered**

C. **as**

D. **whether**

E. **but also**

F. **must either read**

## STYLE

Issues relating to ineffective expression are known as "style" problems. The most common versions on the GMAT are wordiness and passive voice.

**Rule:** On the GMAT, wordiness, redundancy, and unnecessarily passive verbs are wrong.

### Strategy Exercise 6

*Rewrite the following sentences for conciseness.*

   A. The country's procedures for the processing of visas are extremely inefficient.

   B. The shrine is at least 2,000 years old or older.

   C. There are many children who believe in Santa Claus, but there are few adults who do.

### Answers and Explanations

**Note:** The following are the most concise ways of wording each sentence.

   A. **The country's procedures for processing visas are extremely inefficient.**

   B. **The shrine is at least 2,000 years old.**

   C. **Many children believe in Santa Claus, but few adults do.**

# THE METHOD

While there's no substitute for knowing the grammar that Sentence Correction tests, efficient use of your time on Test Day will still require you to work systematically. Look at the three-step method.

## KAPLAN'S 3-STEP METHOD FOR SENTENCE CORRECTIONS:

   **Step 1: Read the original sentence carefully, looking for errors.**

   **Step 2: Scan the answer choices and eliminate those that do not address the error.**

   **Step 3: Evaluate the remaining choices, beginning with the shortest one.**

Let's apply this to the following examples:

1. A recent spate of news reports questioning the long-term health benefits of high-fat diets <u>have done little to convince its practitioners that they should follow more traditional weight-loss plans.</u>

   - ○ have done little to convince its practitioners that they should follow more traditional weight-loss plans.
   - ○ has done little to convince its practitioners to follow more traditional weight-loss plans.
   - ○ have done little to convince their practitioners to follow more traditional weight-loss plans.
   - ○ has done little to convince practitioners of these diets to follow more traditional weight-loss plans.
   - ○ has done little to convince practitioners of these diets they should follow more traditional weight-loss plans.

**Step 1: Read the original sentence carefully, looking for errors.** "A recent spate" is singular, so the verb should be *has*. Thus, you can eliminate **(A)**.

**Step 2: Scan the answer choices and eliminate those that do not address the error.** A quick scan of the choices allows you to eliminate **(C)** as well.

**Step 3: Evaluate the remaining choices, beginning with the shortest one. (B)** can be eliminated because *its* (singular) incorrectly refers back to "high-fat diets" (plural). There doesn't seem to be anything wrong with **(D)** but—for the record—**(E)** is incorrect as you can "convince practitioners **to**" or "convince practitioners **that**" but you cannot "convince practitioners **they**." **(D)** is therefore correct.

2. For over 30 years, Dr. Jane Goodall has conducted field studies of large primate species and <u>shares her findings with the general public in an effort</u> to promote conservation of these species and their habitats.

   - ○ shares her findings with the general public in an effort
   - ○ has shared her findings with the general public so as
   - ○ shared her findings with the general public in an effort
   - ○ will share her findings with the general public so as
   - ○ would share her findings with the general public in an effort

**Step 1: Read the original sentence carefully, looking for errors.** The issue here is parallel structure. ". . . has conducted" needs to be followed by either *shared* or *has shared.* So you can eliminate **(A)**.

**Step 2: Scan the answer choices and eliminate those that do not address the error.** A quick scan eliminates choices **(D)** and **(E)**.

**Step 3: Evaluate the remaining choices, beginning with the shortest one.** **(B)**'s awkward "so as"—which is *never* correct on the GMAT—makes it wrong. **(C)** is correct.

3. Scientists have created a new substance that is <u>so transparent as to be</u> almost invisible.

   ○ so transparent as to be

   ○ so transparent it has been

   ○ so transparent that it was

   ○ transparent enough so that it is

   ○ transparent enough so as to be

**Step 1: Read the original sentence carefully, looking for errors.** You may have thought the strange-sounding "so . . . as to be" idiom is wrong, but this is actually a valid idiom that GMAT writers like using precisely because it sounds wrong to so many ears. There is no error in this sentence, so **(A)** is correct.

For the record, **(B)** and **(C)** are wrong as the verb preceding the underlined portion is the present tense *is.* **(D)** and **(E)** are needlessly wordy and do not improve upon the original.

**Remember:** Not all Sentence Correction sentences need correcting. In fact, the most difficult ones for test takers to get right are those that are correct as written.

Now, try your hand at the following practice Sentence Completions.

# PRACTICE SET

4. The average salary of new jobs <u>is expected to rise in the near future as jobs become available in high-paying industries</u>.

   - ⬭ is expected to rise in the near future as jobs become available in high-paying industries

   - ⬭ are expected to rise in the near future as jobs become available in high-paying industries

   - ⬭ are expected to rise in the near future through jobs becoming available in high-paying industries

   - ⬭ would be expected to rise in the near future through jobs becoming available in high-paying industries

   - ⬭ will rise in the near future because jobs in high-paying industries are expected to become available

5. Cattle were domesticated both for the uses made of the animal—food and leather—<u>but also for</u> the labor the animal could provide.

   - ⬭ but also for

   - ⬭ and for

   - ⬭ or for

   - ⬭ but also

   - ⬭ and also

6. The creation of an independent treasury, establishing lower tariffs, and purchasing the Oregon Territory, all credited to the presidency of James Knox Polk, are among the significant accomplishments that persuade historians to rank this former governor of Tennessee highly as a U.S. president.

   ○ The creation of an independent treasury, securing lower tariffs, and purchasing

   ○ The creation of an independent treasury, securing lower tariffs as well as purchasing

   ○ The creation of an independent treasury, the establishment of lower tariffs, and the purchase of

   ○ Creating an independent treasury, securing lower tariffs, and purchasing

   ○ Creating an independent treasury, the securing of lower tariffs, and the purchasing of

7. Despite the platform of the Republican Party supporting the measure, they keep voting against campaign finance reform in Congress.

   ○ the platform of the Republican Party supporting the measure, they keep voting

   ○ the Republican Party's platform supporting the measure, they keep voting

   ○ the Republicans' platform supporting the measure, it keeps voting

   ○ the Republican Party's platform supporting the measure, party members keep voting

   ○ the supporting measure of the platform of the Republican party, they keep voting

8. Nineteenth-century authors often included encyclopedic information in their novels; Melville's famous chapter of the physiology on whales, contained as it is in his masterwork *Moby Dick*, serves as a perfect example of this phenomenon.

   ○ contained as it is in

   ○ contained as it is within

   ○ contained in

   ○ found contained in

   ○ being found contained in

9. Pablo Picasso's genius is only fully revealed when one considers the various facets of his work as they developed through many artistic phases, <u>beginning with his Red period, continuing through his Blue period, and finishing with his period of Cubism</u>.

   ○ beginning with his Red period, continuing through his Blue period, and finishing with his period of Cubism

   ○ beginning with his Red period, continuing through his Blue period, and finishing with his Cubist period

   ○ beginning with his Red period, and continuing through his Blue period and his Cubist period

   ○ beginning with his Red period phase, his Blue period phase, and his phase of Cubism

   ○ beginning with his Red period, his Blue period, and his period of Cubism

10. The significant number of overtime and weekend hours accumulated by many employees in order to compensate for overly optimistic deadlines <u>lend validity to the observation that many of the firm's top managers still pine for the era of the six-day workweek</u>.

   ○ lend validity to the observation that many of the firm's top managers still pine for the era of the six-day workweek

   ○ lends validity to the observation of many of the firm's top managers' still pining for the era of the six-day workweek

   ○ lends validity to the observation of many of the firm's top managers, still pining for the six-day workweek era

   ○ lend it validity to observe that many of the firm's top managers still pine for the era of the six-day workweek

   ○ lends validity to the observation that many of the firm's top managers still pine for the era of the six-day workweek

11. In many coastal New England towns, <u>the fisherman still operates as they have</u> for generations, displaying and selling their catch dockside at the end of each day.

   ○ the fisherman still operates as they have

   ○ the fisherman still operates as was done

   ○ fishermen still operate as they have done

   ○ the fisherman still operates as he has

   ○ fishermen still operate as they had

12. Recent surveys indicate that, contrary to popular belief, total abstinence from alcohol does not correlate <u>as strongly with good health as does moderate drinking</u>.

   ○ as strongly with good health as does moderate drinking

   ○ strongly with good health, like moderate drinking does

   ○ as strongly with good health as does moderately drinking

   ○ as strongly with good health as with moderate drinking

   ○ as strongly with good health as moderate drinking

13. The experts from the Fish and Wildlife Department could not decide which one of eight possible nesting sites along the Platte River <u>will provide the best habitat</u> into which to release the cranes.

   ○ will provide the best habitat

   ○ would be providing the better habitat

   ○ would provide the better habitat

   ○ would provide the best habitat

   ○ is providing the best habitat

14. Several stock market analysts now report that the plummeting <u>values of many
    high-tech stocks have fallen so as to make</u> them once again attractive to investors.

    ○ values of many high-tech stocks have fallen so as to make

    ○ high-tech stock values have fallen, making

    ○ descent of many high-tech stock values have made

    ○ values of many high-tech stocks are making

    ○ values of many high-tech stocks have fallen, which has made

15. Due to the limitations imposed by the speed of light, the visible universe <u>is
    estimated as</u> a mere fraction of the total universe.

    ○ is estimated as

    ○ is estimated to be

    ○ is estimated at

    ○ estimated to be

    ○ estimated at

16. The macabre subject matter of Macbeth, together with the widespread belief that
    real-life tragedies have accompanied many productions, <u>has made the name of
    the play so dreaded that not even the least superstitious members of most casts
    will utter</u> it.

    ○ has made the name of the play so dreaded that not even the least
      superstitious members of most casts will utter

    ○ have made the play's name so dreaded, even the least superstitious of most
      cast members will not utter

    ○ have made the play's name sufficiently dreaded, so that even the less
      superstitious members of most casts will not utter

    ○ have made the name of the play sufficiently dreaded, so that not even the
      least superstitious members of most casts will utter

    ○ has made it that the name of the play is dreaded, so that not even the least
      superstitious members of most casts will utter

17.  Unlike <u>its fellow Baltic nations, Latvia and Lithuania, the economy of Estonia grew at an astonishing rate in the late '90s, and at the end of the decade it was placed on the fast track to join</u> the European Union.

   ○ its fellow Baltic nations, Latvia and Lithuania, the economy of Estonia grew at an astonishing rate in the late '90s, and at the end of the decade it was placed on the fast track to join

   ○ its fellow Baltic nations, Latvia and Lithuania, Estonia's economy grew at an astonishing rate in the late '90s, and at the end of the decade was placed on the fast track to join

   ○ its fellow Baltic nations, Latvia and Lithuania, Estonia's economy grew at an astonishing rate in the late '90s, and at the end of the decade they were placed on the fast track to join

   ○ Latvia and Lithuania, its fellow Baltic nations, the economy of Estonia grew at an astonishing rate in the late '90s, and at the end of the decade was placed on the fast track to join

   ○ Latvia and Lithuania, its fellow Baltic nations, Estonia possessed an economy that grew at an astonishing rate in the late '90s, and at the end of the decade the country was placed on the fast track to join

18.  The ancient Sumerians are credited <u>as having</u> created the first phonetic writing system as long ago as 3100 BCE.

   ○ as having

   ○ to have

   ○ for having

   ○ with having

   ○ as being the ones who

19. <u>By the number of carbons in the compound's longest chain, a hydrocarbon's standard name is partly determined.</u>

    ○ By the number of carbons in the compound's longest chain, a hydrocarbon's standard name is partly determined

    ○ The number of carbons in the compound's longest continuous chain enables partial determination of the standard name of a hydrocarbon

    ○ The standard name of a hydrocarbon is partly determined by the number of carbons in the compound's longest continuous chain

    ○ Counting the number of carbons in the compound's longest continuous chain enables partially determining a hydrocarbon's standard name

    ○ As the carbons on a hydrocarbon's longest continuous chain are counted, so that partially determines the compound's standard name

20. Even inexperienced art history students can identify works of the Impressionist painters by both their characteristic brushwork and, equally revolutionary in the late nineteenth century, <u>because they preferred to use brights and pastels.</u>

    ○ because they preferred to use brights and pastels

    ○ their preference for brights and pastels

    ○ they preferred to use brights and pastels

    ○ by the preference that they showed for brights and pastels

    ○ by their preference for brights and pastels

21. The new software program allows accounting clerks to update the expense log on a daily basis, <u>resulting in preparing monthly expense reports now taking only one-fifth as long to calculate and process than</u> before.

    ◯ resulting in preparing monthly expense reports now taking only one-fifth as long to calculate and process than

    ◯ resulting in them now spending only one-fifth the time calculating and processing monthly expense reports of what they did

    ◯ resulting in them now spending only one-fifth the time calculating and processing monthly expense reports than they did

    ◯ and they now spend only one-fifth as much time as a result calculating and processing monthly expense reports than

    ◯ and as a result, clerks now spend only one-fifth as much time calculating and processing monthly expense reports as they did

22. After migrating to Tasmania, <u>Bass Strait's rising waters prevented the return of a group of Aborigines</u> to the Australian mainland.

    ◯ Bass Strait's rising waters prevented the return of a group of Aborigines

    ◯ with its rising waters, Bass Strait prevented the return of a group of Aborigines

    ◯ a group of Aborigines was prevented by the rising waters of Bass Strait from returning

    ◯ the rising waters of Bass Strait prevented the return of a group of Aborigines

    ◯ Bass Strait with its rising waters prevented a group of Aborigines from returning

23. If the conclusions drawn in Dr. Pelletier's report on the analgesic's effect on children are correct, <u>ingesting the same dosage as is commonly ingested by adults may result in permanent paralysis in some children, whose</u> smaller bodies can tolerate the drug only in minute quantities.

    - ⬭ ingesting the same dosage as is commonly ingested by adults may result in permanent paralysis in some children, whose

    - ⬭ it may result in permanent paralysis for some children to ingest the same dosage as adults do; their

    - ⬭ permanent paralysis may result from ingesting the same dosage as adults commonly do by some children, whose

    - ⬭ permanent paralysis may result for some children from ingesting the same dosage as adults commonly ingest; their

    - ⬭ some children ingesting the same dosage as is commonly ingested by adults may result in permanent paralysis; their

24. Records of the first 736 British convicts deported to Australia reveal <u>convictions for crimes against property in all cases, and they ranged</u> from highway robbery to forgery.

    - ⬭ convictions for crimes against property in all cases, and they ranged

    - ⬭ convictions in all cases were for crimes against property and ranging

    - ⬭ the ranging of convictions for crimes against property in all cases

    - ⬭ that all were convicted of crimes against property, ranging

    - ⬭ that all of them had convictions for crimes that were against property; the range was

25. Fossils found recently in Pakistan provide evidence <u>supporting the theory of land mammals returning to the water that later</u> evolved into modern whales.

   ○ supporting the theory of land mammals returning to the water that later

   ○ supporting the theory that, after returning to the water, land mammals

   ○ that supports the theory of land mammals that returned to the water and that later

   ○ in support of the theory that land mammals returned to the water and that they later

   ○ of support for the theory of land mammals that returned to the water and after

# THE WRAP-UP

Doing well on Sentence Correction requires the following:

- Knowing the five rules of GMAT grammar—

   1. **Verb usage** (proper agreement and correct tense)

   2. **Reference** (proper use of pronouns and modifiers)

   3. **Parallel structure** (consistency among items in a list or comparison)

   4. **Idioms** (proper use of idiomatic expressions)

   5. **Style** (avoiding excess verbiage, using active verbs, etc.)

- Approaching problems systematically

- Keeping the following in mind—

   1. Choice **(A)** will always repeat the original, so never waste time reading it.

   2. Some problems will be correct as written. These usually involve seemingly awkward constructions that are actually grammatically correct.

   3. There is no substitute for knowing the rules of English grammar, style, and usage.

# ANSWERS AND EXPLANATIONS

## 4. (A)

The subject is *salary,* so the verb should be singular, which eliminates **(B)** and **(C)**. As written, "is expected to rise in the near future" makes good sense; there's no need to complicate the verb tense, as **(D)** does. **(E)** scrambles the meaning of the sentence, turning an expectation into a fact.

## 5. (B)

*Both* sets up the "both *A* and *B*" construction, so we need an *and* to follow. This eliminates everything except choices **(B)** and **(E)**. **(E)**'s "and also" cannot parallel "both for," so **(B)** is correct.

## 6. (C)

The underlined portion contains a list, so check for consistency among the items. Of the choices, only **(C)** and **(D)** consist of lists that are parallel. Because the list is supposed to refer to achievements, the nouns in **(C)** make more sense than the gerunds in **(D)**, so **(C)** is correct.

## 7. (D)

Be suspicious any time you see *they* or *it* in the underlined portion of the sentence or among the answer choices. **(A)**, **(B)**, and **(E)** are out because there is no antecedent plural noun to which *they* could be referring. **(C)** has the platform doing the voting in Congress. Only **(D)** avoids these pronoun pitfalls.

## 8. (C)

The underlined portion is grammatically correct but seems a bit wordy. **(C)** is the most concise choice and doesn't introduce any errors, so it is correct.

## 9. (B)

The underlined portion contains a list, so make sure the terms are consistent. Eliminate choices **(A)**, **(D)**, and **(E)**, as each contains a list that isn't parallel. **(B)** and **(C)** have consistent lists, but **(C)** loses the sequential sense contained in the original sentence, so **(B)** is correct.

### 10. (E)

The subject is not *hours,* but *the number,* which requires a singular verb. If you didn't see that up front, a quick vertical scan of each choice shows that subject-verb agreement is at issue. *The number* goes with the singular verb *lends* in choices (**B**), (**C**), and (**E**), so you can eliminate (**A**) and (**D**). It's not the observation of many managers that's under discussion; rather, it's the observation that many managers pine for a six-day workweek. That makes (**E**) correct.

### 11. (C)

You have to read the entire sentence to know whether to go singular or plural here. Because the sentence refers to "their catch," you need plural *fishermen* and plural *they.* That eliminates everything but (**C**) and (**E**). Because the fishermen have been operating the same way "for generations" and they still operate that way, the proper verb tense is present perfect, which makes (**C**) correct.

### 12. (A)

The underlined portion contains part of a comparison, so begin by ensuring that the comparison is appropriate. The noun phrase "moderate drinking" is being correctly compared to "total abstinence." (**B**) and (**D**) mangle the sense of that comparison, while (**C**) breaks the parallel. (**E**) can also be eliminated because the second verb, *does,* is necessary to convey the sense that the comparison is between how one correlates and how the other correlates. That leaves the original as the correct answer.

### 13. (D)

The part of the sentence that isn't underlined is in past tense, so you need to use *would* to indicate a reference to the future made in the past. Eliminate (**A**) and (**E**). Of the remaining choices, (**B**) and (**C**) incorrectly use *better* when there are eight nesting sites (*better* can only be used when comparing two things), so (**D**) is correct.

### 14. (D)

*Plummeting* means falling, so using the two of them together is redundant. That eliminates (**A**), (**B**), and (**E**). (**C**) can also be eliminated for its "plummeting descent." Only (**D**) manages to avoid the redundancy trap, so it is correct.

### 15. (B)

The correct idiom is "estimated to be," which eliminates **(A)**, **(C)**, and **(E)**. **(D)** loses the crucial verb *is*, so it is out as well. That leaves **(B)**, the correct answer.

### 16. (A)

When a subject is separated from its verb, you must check that the two agree. "The macabre subject matter of Macbeth" is singular, so the singular *has* should be used. Eliminate **(B)**, **(C)**, and **(D)**. The pronoun *it* in **(E)** has no clear antecedent, and the phrase "has made it that" is awkward, so the original wording is correct.

### 17. (E)

Be on the lookout for modifying phrases followed by commas at the beginning of a sentence. In this case, all the sentences begin with variations of "Unlike its fellow Baltic nations, Latvia and Lithuania," so what follows this introduction should in fact be a Baltic nation—i.e., Estonia—not Estonia's economy. Only **(E)** corrects this misplaced modifier error.

### 18. (D)

The correct idiom is "credited with." Only **(D)** addresses this error.

### 19. (C)

When the entire sentence is underlined, style problems are often found in many of the answer choices, so read and eliminate aggressively. **(A)** needlessly complicates the sentence by sticking the long and confusing prepositional phrase "By the number . . ." at the beginning of the sentence. (It's also a misplaced modifier, as the phrase should be next to *determined*.) **(B)**'s "enables partial determination of the standard name" is needlessly wordy. **(D)**'s "enables partially determining" is extremely awkward, and **(E)** isn't even a complete sentence. Only **(C)** avoids these problems, making it the correct answer.

### 20. (B)

"Both . . . and" is a common GMAT construction that links similar terms, so be ready to check for parallel structure. The word *their* follows *both,* so the word that follows *and* must parallel *their.* Only **(B)** does that correctly.

### 21. (E)

A modifier, like the underlined phrase here, attaches itself to the noun to which it's closest, so the original sentence says the *basis* is "resulting in preparing monthly expense reports now taking only one-fifth as long to calculate as before." Logically this doesn't work, so eliminate choices **(A)**, **(B)**, and **(C)** for this error. **(D)** can also be thrown out, as *they* has no clear antecedent noun. That leaves **(E)** as the correct answer.

### 22. (C)

The sentence begins with the modifying phrase "After migrating to Tasmania," so what follows must be whoever (or whatever) did the migrating. The only choice that makes sense is **(C)**, as neither "Bass Strait" nor its "rising waters" can do any migrating.

### 23. (A)

Here's a classic example of a sentence that doesn't sound particularly appealing in its original form but is nonetheless grammatically correct. A quick scan of the choices reveals a clear split between *whose* and *their*. The way the sentence is written, grammatically, "their (smaller bodies)" could refer to "adults' (bodies)" or "children's (bodies)." That's too ambiguous for the GMAT, so eliminate **(B)**, **(D)**, and **(E)**. **(C)**'s "by some children" seems to modify how the adults ingest the dosage, so it's out as well. Only the original remains, and it is correct.

### 24. (D)

The underlined portion seems awkward and needlessly wordy, so begin by checking the shortest choice. **(D)** is nice and concise, making it the correct answer. **(B)**'s "and ranging," **(C)**'s "the ranging of convictions," and **(E)**'s "the range was" are all awkward and verbose.

### 25. (B)

The "theory of land mammals . . ." is not idiomatically correct in context (i.e., you have a theory of evolution but a theory that animals evolve.) That eliminates **(A)**, **(C)**, and **(E)**. **(D)** has the unnecessary words "that they," so **(B)** is correct.

# CHAPTER 6: READING COMPREHENSION

The GMAT's Verbal section contains four Reading Comprehension passages. There are two shorter passages with 3 questions each and two longer passages with 4 questions each for a total of 14 questions out of the 41 total questions in the Verbal section, making them a bit over one-third of your Verbal subscore.

The number of passages makes Reading Comprehension the most time-consuming question type and—for many test takers—the most intimidating portion of the Verbal section. As you'll see in this chapter, this need not be the case.

Despite what many test takers seem to believe, Reading Comprehension questions do not test your ability to read and comprehend a passage so thoroughly that you practically memorize what you read. Nor do they test your ability to relate what you read to outside knowledge. Furthermore, they most definitely do not test your ability to offer a creative or original analysis of what you read.

What Reading Comprehension questions do test is your ability to understand the gist of the passage and, where necessary, to research the passage for specific information to answer the question before you. Developing a method for handling Reading Comprehension questions quickly so that you don't get bogged down reading and rereading the passages will help you do well on this question type.

The directions for the Reading Comprehension passage set will look like this:

> **Directions:** The questions in this group are based on the content of the passage. After reading the passage, answer each question accompanying it on the basis of what's stated or implied.

The passage will be visible on one side of the monitor as long as you have a question on that passage. You will see only one question at a time on the monitor, and you will have to answer each question before you can see the next question. If the text is longer than the available space, you'll be given a scroll bar to move through it.

GMAT Reading Comprehension questions must be answered with information from the passage alone. You may interpret what the content implies, but you **cannot** use outside knowledge.

Reading Comprehension passages are written in dense, often technical, prose and are adapted from books and journals in the broad areas of business, the social sciences, and the natural sciences. You can expect to get at least one of each type of passage on the GMAT you take.

The majority of GMAT Reading Comprehension questions come in two flavors:

1. Global questions, which ask general questions about the passage
2. Detail questions, which require you to locate information in the passage to answer very specific questions

GMAT Reading Comprehension wrong answer choices are always drawn from a limited list of predictable wrong answer types. We'll be reviewing those later in this chapter.

# THE STRATEGY

Reading Comprehension is an open-book test. All the answers are right there in the passage, so the one factor that separates the great from the mediocre is time: those who make good use of it score well, while those who squander it do poorly. Because proper time management is the key to a great score, the strategy we advise depends on the amount of time you have left.

## IF YOU'RE PACING YOURSELF SUCCESSFULLY

If you're doing well in terms of time, you can afford to approach the reading passages with the following principles in mind. It should take you no more than two minutes to dissect the passage and to grasp its main idea.

## Look for the Topic, Scope, Purpose, Main Idea, and Tone

The GMAT is a "thinking" test, and that fact is just as true in Reading Comprehension as it is in any other section. The test makers are mainly interested in your understanding of the *why* and the *how*—*why* something is written and *how* the passage was put together. There is little interest in testing what is being written on the page because anyone who can read can answer that (business schools are a *bit* pickier than that!).

Focusing instead on the topic, scope, purpose, main idea, and tone will help you gain a far better understanding of the passage and zoom in on the right answers. The passage's topic is broadly stated (e.g., solving world hunger). The scope is narrower (e.g., a new technology is needed for solving world hunger).

You also need to decipher the author's tone—the attitude he or she takes toward the subject matter. You also must differentiate between the author's own opinions and other people's opinions. GMAT authors can disagree with other people, but they won't contradict themselves.

It's the opinions and theories that the Reading Comp passages are built on, and you should pay the most attention to them.

Once you spot opinion or theory, you can step back from the barrage of words and attack the passage critically, saying, "Okay, but where is the support for this idea? Does the author agree or disagree?" That will also help you identify the structure of the passage, or how the author has organized his or her ideas.

Put together, the passage's structure and its opinions/theories (especially the author's) will lead you to understand the main idea of the passage and the author's primary purpose in writing the passage. This is critical, as most GMAT passages have questions that involve these two aspects directly. Every passage boils down to one main idea, and the main idea and purpose of the passage are intertwined. Take, for example, the hypothetical passage in which the topic was solving world hunger and the scope was a new technology for solving world hunger. The author's main idea could be that biochemical engineering is a new technology that can help solve world hunger. The author's primary idea and subjective purpose would then be simply a restatement of this main idea in a more general way: to describe a new technology and its promising uses.

## Identify Key Words

Reading Comp passages are full of structural signals—key words or phrases that help the author string ideas together logically. They allow you to infer a great deal about content, even if that content is obscure or difficult.

Conclusion signals *(therefore, consequently, thus)* and evidence signals *(because, since)* are extremely helpful, as are contrast keywords *(but, however, although, by contrast),* which indicate an opposition or shift in ideas. These help you map out the passage's structure.

Emphasis/opinion signals *(most of all, critical, especially, ironically, very)* are words or phrases that an author uses to say, "Here's what I consider important or significant!" Not only do emphasis/opinion signals help you build your road map, but they also allow you to anticipate what information in the passage will be tested in the questions.

All authors use key words. However, authors of Reading Comprehension passages use them with special frequency, largely as a way of rewarding strategic readers.

## Don't Sweat the Details

Details exist in passages to support and flesh out the author's claims. Note their purpose as you quickly read over them but do not waste your time mulling over their exact content, as that will not contribute to your overall understanding of the passage's structure.

## Create a Road Map As You Read

Creating a road map as you read will allow you to research the passage quickly when a particular question calls for it. There's no point in using key words and identifying the topic, scope, main idea, purpose, and tone of the passage if you can't refer back to them quickly to answer test questions!

## IF YOU'RE REALLY LOW ON TIME

Late in the Verbal section, if you have next to no time left, try to circle as many key words as you can. Also, concentrate on looking for the main idea of the passage by focusing on the first and last sentences of each paragraph.

This strategy will not always work, and it is only meant as an absolute last resort. Nevertheless, if you are faced with either a main idea or primary purpose question, these two sentences statistically have the highest chance of containing both.

# THE METHOD

Following is a sample passage. Apply Kaplan's four-step method as you go along.

## KAPLAN'S 4-STEP METHOD FOR READING COMPREHENSION:

**Step 1:** Read the passage strategically and create a road map.

**Step 2:** Read the question stem.

**Step 3:** Prephrase an answer, going back to the passage for research if necessary.

**Step 4:** Attack the answer choices, choosing the one that best matches your prephrase.

**Step 1: Read the passage strategically and create a road map.**

To the historian of ideas interested in examining the relationship between an era's scientific thought and its social milieu, the late-nineteenth-century "discovery" of a new radiation by the Frenchman Gustave LeBon presents a fascinating case study. LeBon, an amateur
(5) scientist, made a report in which he claimed to have found that ordinary light from an oil lamp produced invisible radiation as it impinged upon a closed metal box and that this radiation affected a photographic plate inside the box producing an image of another plate in the box. He called this new radiation "black light" and deemed it some sort
(10) of extraordinary vibration capable of penetrating opaque objects and intermediate in nature between light and electricity.

LeBon's radiation entered the memoirs of the French Academy of Sciences alongside Roentgen's X-rays and Becquerel's uranium rays and excited vehement debate for a decade. This debate ended only
(15) after Auguste Lumière proved that the phenomenon could be produced without the intervention of light and in fact originated in improper chemical preparation of the plates themselves. Yet until then, the experiments and ideas of LeBon, an outsider to the universities and lycées of France, were taken quite seriously by many members of the
(20) scientific elite.

The ready acceptance of LeBon's ideas by the scientific establishment of his day was in part due to the internal upheaval in physical theory at the end of the nineteenth century. It was also

assisted by his personal friendships with several members of the
(25) Academy. Most important, his success lay in his interpretation of black
light, which used terminology that drew on the prevalent intellectual
and philosophical trends of his time: an antirationalism and,
particularly, an antimaterialism that emphasized spontaneity, evolution,
and action at the expense of the traditional emphasis in science on
(30) mechanism, determinism, and materialism.

1. Which one of the following best expresses the main idea of the
   passage?

   ⬭ LeBon's black light radiation, which was taken seriously
   by his contemporaries, was actually a misinterpretation of
   experimental evidence.

   ⬭ LeBon's scientific work was accepted by the French Academy of
   Sciences primarily because little was known about radiation at
   that time.

   ⬭ The French Academy's acceptance of LeBon's discovery was the
   result of the unusually strong influence intellectuals had on the
   progress of science in the nineteenth century.

   ⬭ LeBon's nineteenth-century "discovery" of black light illustrates
   the ways in which culture can impact the acceptance of
   scientific theory.

   ⬭ The acceptance of LeBon's theories demonstrates the fact that
   the primary factor in the success of a scientific theory lies in its
   social milieu.

**Step 2: Read the question stem.** This is a "main idea" Global question. To answer it,
you will need to focus on the big picture.

**Step 3: Prephrase an answer, going back to the passage for research if necessary.**
Reading for authorial intent and making your road map as you read will allow you to
tackle Global questions without having to go back to the passage for research.

The first sentence in the passage indicates that LeBon's "discovery" of a new radiation
is of interest because it illustrates the ways in which scientific thought interacts with
social milieu (i.e., the culture at large).

**Step 4: Attack the answer choices, choosing the one that best matches your prephrase.** (D) matches our prediction and is correct. Common wrong answer choices to Global questions do one or more of the following:

- **They are too specific, focusing on just one portion of the passage.** (A) takes a very small truth from the passage (in this case, from paragraph 2) and tries to pass it off as the main idea. Constantly reading for authorial intent will allow you handily to sidestep these traps.

- **They are too broad, going beyond the scope of the passage.** (E) focuses on "the success of a scientific theory" when the passage only deals with a theory's acceptance. Right answers must be derivable from the passage alone, so choices that step beyond its contents cannot be correct.

- **They are too strongly worded.** Correct answers to GMAT Reading Comprehension questions tend to feature wishy-washy wording (such as *could*, *probably*, *sometimes*, and *may*), so be wary of any choice that contains extreme language, such as (E)'s "primary factor." Extreme wording isn't automatically wrong: it's only wrong when the passage's language isn't equally certain—which will often be the case.

- **They misrepresent or contradict the passage.** This is yet another type of wrong answer that reading for authorial intent will allow you to avoid. (C) misrepresents the reasons for the acceptance of LeBon's theories, while (B) flat out contradicts the final paragraph.

The answer is (D).

2. Which of the following is NOT given as a reason why LeBon's black light theory was accepted as reasonable?

- ◯ Given the knowledge of the time, it provided a plausible explanation of a reported phenomenon.

- ◯ It was couched in terms that reflected the prevailing inclinations in thought.

- ◯ It was posited at a time when arguments between scientists on the nature of radiation had not yet been settled.

- ◯ LeBon concealed imperfections in his method.

- ◯ LeBon was friends with members of the scientific establishment.

**Step 2: Read the question stem.** This is a Detail question. Detail questions ask about a specific part of the passage.

**Step 3: Prephrase an answer, going back to the passage for research if necessary.** Reading with the author's purpose in mind means *not* paying too much attention to the details, so you should expect to need to research the answer for this type of question.

This particular question wants the one answer that is *not* stated or implied, so the best way to answer it is by eliminating the ones that *are* in the passage.

**Step 4: Attack the answer choices, choosing the one that best matches your prephrase.** You can eliminate **(B)**, **(C)**, and **(E)**, as they all paraphrase portions of the final paragraph. **(A)** isn't directly stated, but it is implied: LeBon's theories would not have been taken seriously for a decade if they did not offer a plausible explanation of a reported phenomenon given the knowledge of the time. Only **(D)** does not appear in any shape or form, as whether or not LeBon "deliberately concealed imperfections" is beyond the scope of the passage. Common wrong answer choices to Detail questions do one or more of the following:

- **They refer to the wrong part of the passage.** This is a very common trap that can be difficult to avoid if you do not research your answers. This wrong answer choice presents a genuine detail from the passage—just not one to which the question relates.

- **They misrepresent the passage.** As in Global questions, choices that distort the meaning of the original text can show up in Detail questions as well.

- **They are too broad, going beyond the scope of the passage.** Correct answers (or in questions like this one, incorrect answers) to Detail questions are almost always *paraphrases* of information contained in the passage and cannot go beyond its scope.

- **They are too strongly worded.** Extreme wording applies to Detail questions as well, so be on the lookout for this.

The answer is **(D)**.

3. The acceptance of which of the following beliefs is most closely analogous to acceptance of LeBon's theories as described by the author?

○ Although initially rejected, the genetic theories of Lysenko were forced on academics in the U.S.S.R. because of his connections within the Soviet government.

○ Because religion placed the Earth at the center of all things, medieval scholars refused to consider other possibilities.

○ Although based on flawed images, Lowell's claims for Martian canals gained acceptance for a time due to widespread fascination with the possibility of extraterrestrial life.

○ Astrology gains its authority by producing a great number of vague predictions, some of which can be interpreted as true.

○ Wegener's theory of continental drift seemed initially plausible to many but only became accepted after bitter controversy over the geological evidence.

**Step 2: Read the question stem.** This is an analogous situation question. Analogous situation questions ask for the answer choice that describes a situation most similar to the one in the passage.

**Step 3: Prephrase an answer, going back to the passage for research if necessary.** Prephrasing the answer to this type of question involves putting the situation or principle from the passage into your own words.

In this case, while LeBon's theories were wrong, they were accepted for a time primarily because they concurred with the cultural trends of his day.

**Step 4: Attack the answer choices, choosing the one that best matches your prephrase.** Scanning the choices with our paraphrase in mind, you'll notice that **(C)** matches up perfectly: Lowell's images were flawed, but his claims were accepted for a time because the popular culture of his day was fascinated with the possibility of extraterrestrial life. Common wrong answer choices will deviate from this prephrase in at least one way:

LeBon's theories faced neither the initial rejection in **(A)** nor the eventual acceptance in **(E)**. **(B)** misses out on the acceptance of theories, and **(D)** completely misses the mark.

The answer is **(C)**.

Let's try another passage.

**Step 1: Read the passage strategically and create a road map.** Using the techniques discussed in the strategy section, read strategically and road-map this passage.

> Congress has had numerous opportunities in recent years to
> reconsider the arrangements under which federal forest lands are
> owned and managed. New institutional structures merit development
> because federal forest lands cannot be efficiently managed under the
> (5) hierarchical structure that now exists. The system is too complex to be
> understood by any single authority. The establishment of each forest
> as an independent public corporation would simplify the management
> structure and promote greater efficiency, control, and accountability.
>      To illustrate how a system for independent public corporations might
> (10) work, consider the National Forest System. Each National Forest would
> become an independent public corporation, operating under a federal
> charter giving it legal authority to manage land. The charter would
> give the corporation the right to establish its own production goals,
> land uses, management practices, and financial arrangements within
> (15) the policy constraints set by the Public Corporations Board. To ensure
> economic efficiency in making decisions, the Public Corporations Board
> would establish a minimum average rate of return to be earned on
> assets held by each corporation. Each corporation would be required to
> organize a system for reporting revenues, costs, capital investments and
> (20) recovery, profits, and the other standard measures of financial health.
> While the financial objective would not necessarily be to maximize profit,
> there would be a requirement to earn at least a public utility rate of
> return on the resources under the corporation's control.
>      Such an approach to federal land management would encourage
> (25) greater efficiency in the utilization of land, capital, and labor. This
> approach could also promote a more stable workforce. A positive
> program of advancement, more flexible job classifications, professional
> training, and above all, the ability to counter outside bids with higher

salary would enable a corporation to retain its best workers. A third
(30)   advantage to this approach is that federal land management would
become less vulnerable to the politics of special interest groups.

4. The primary purpose of this passage is to

○ suggest that the National Forest System is plagued by many
problems.

○ argue that it is necessary to restructure the management of
federal forest lands.

○ insist that private corporations be allowed to manage the
country's natural resources.

○ discuss the role of private corporations in the management
of the National Forest System.

○ highlight the competing needs of public agencies managing
national resources.

**Step 2: Read the question stem.** This is a primary purpose Global question. To
answer it, focus on *why* the author wrote the passage.

**Step 3: Prephrase an answer, going back to the passage for research if necessary.**
The answer choices in primary purpose questions will often begin with verbs. The best
way to handle these is to predict a verb, then use a "vertical scan" to eliminate choices
that won't work.

The main idea of this passage is clearly found in the first paragraph: managing forests
as public corporations would have several advantages over the present system. The
author's purpose is to advocate this system.

**Step 4: Attack the answer choices, choosing the one that best matches your
prephrase.** (**B**) captures our prephrase perfectly. As with main idea Global questions,
each of the wrong choices goes wrong in predictable ways. The author does mention the
problems referred to in (**A**), but the focus of the passage is the solution. (**C**) and (**D**)
refer to private corporations—never discussed in the passage—and (**E**) goes beyond the
scope of the passage, referring to the competing needs of various agencies managing
national resources while the passage discusses only the National Forest System.

The answer is (**B**).

5. The author suggests that administrators of federal forest lands have been handicapped by which of the following?

○ The public expectation that federal forest lands will remain undeveloped

○ The failure of environmental experts to investigate the problems of federal forest lands

○ The inability of the federal government to compete with private corporations for the services of skilled professionals

○ The unwillingness of Congress to pass laws to protect federal forest lands from private developers

○ The difficulty of persuading citizens to invest their capital in a government-run endeavor

**Step 2: Read the question stem.** This is an Inference question. Despite the wishy-washy wording (in this case, asking what the passage *suggests*), Inference questions ask for what *must be true* based on the passage. While you will be reading between the lines, correct answers will *never* require a major reach.

**Step 3: Prephrase an answer, going back to the passage for research if necessary.** Most of the passage talks directly or indirectly about forest management problems, so a prephrase is all but impossible. Instead, let's attack the choices directly.

**Step 4: Attack the answer choices, choosing the one that best matches your prephrase.** **(A)**, **(B)**, **(D)**, and **(E)** can be thrown out, as "public expectation," "failure of environment experts to investigate," "the unwillingness of Congress to pass laws," and "the difficulty of persuading citizens to invest" are never mentioned anywhere in the passage. **(C)**, however, corresponds to the personnel issue referenced in the final paragraph:

> A positive program of advancement, more flexible job classifications, professional training, and above all, the ability to counter outside bids with higher salary would enable a corporation to retain its best workers.

Hence, it doesn't take much inferring to conclude that present administrators are hampered by the inability to compete with private corporations for the services of skilled professionals. Common wrong answer choices to Inference questions do one or more of the following:

- **They go beyond the scope of the passage.** Wrong answer choices to Inference questions will often introduce things that the passage provides no information on.

- **They are too strongly worded.** Extreme wording applies to many types of questions but *especially* to Inference questions.

- **They misrepresent or contradict the passage.** As with main idea questions, wrong answer choices in Inference are susceptible to misrepresentation and/or contradiction.

The answer is **(C)**.

6. The author's attitude toward the "hierarchical structure" mentioned in line 5 can best be characterized as

   ⬭ resigned.

   ⬭ admiring.

   ⬭ skeptical.

   ⬭ bitter.

   ⬭ ambivalent.

**Step 2: Read the question stem.** This is an author's attitude question. Such questions can either ask for the author's tone throughout the passage (Global) or in one specific spot (Detail).

**Step 3: Prephrase an answer, going back to the passage for research if necessary.** Author's attitude questions are a gift, as simply figuring out whether the author's tone is positive or negative will usually allow you to eliminate a healthy number of choices. This question was generous enough to provide a line reference, so make use of it!

Paragraph 1 cites "hierarchical structure" as *the basic problem*. Thus, the answer here must be negative—strongly negative—but in keeping with the passage's unemotional tone.

**Step 4: Attack the answer choices, choosing the one that best matches your prephrase. (B)** is too positive while **(D)** sounds too emotional, so both can be eliminated right away. **(A)** is out because the author is not resigned—he's *advocating* a change. **(E)** is also wrong because it implies mixed feelings, some positive, some negative. That leaves **(C)**, which is both negative and purposeful.

The answer is **(C)**.

7. Which of the following best describes the organization of the passage?

   ○ A proposal is made, and then supporting arguments are set forth.

   ○ One claim is evaluated and then rejected in favor of another claim.

   ○ A point of view is stated, and then evidence for and against it is evaluated.

   ○ A problem is outlined, and then various solutions are discussed.

   ○ Opposing opinions are introduced and then debated.

**Step 2: Read the question stem.** This is a structure Global question. This type of question asks for a 1:1 matchup between the passage and the correct choice.

**Step 3: Prephrase an answer, going back to the passage for research if necessary.** Structure questions are your reward for creating a proper road map, as they can usually be answered simply by referring to it.

If you had created a road map by taking brief notes about the paragraphs as you read through the passage, it might have looked like this—paragraph 1: *need better forest mgmt*; paragraph 2: *how pub corps work*; and paragraph 3: *advantages*. In any case, the organization could be summarized as follows: a proposed solution, detailed explanation of solution, and finally some advantages.

**Step 4: Attack the answer choices, choosing the one that best matches your prephrase.** **(A)** matches our prephrase. Note how each of the wrong answers has wording that makes it clearly wrong. The author evaluates a claim or proposal, as in **(B)**, but never *rejects* it for another. **(C)** is off because the author never gives evidence *against* the proposal. Nor does he mention other *solutions* or *opposing opinions* in **(D)** and **(E)**, respectively.

The answer is **(A)**.

**Remember:** Wrong answers in GMAT Reading Comprehension questions will always have something—a word, a phrase, and so on—*purposely inserted* to make them wrong. They will never be wrong by accident, so learning to recognize the different types of wrong answers is just as important as learning to pick out the correct one.

Try your hand at the following passages.

# PRACTICE SET

The search for an explanation of the historically weak status of U.S. third-party movements is illuminated by examining the conditions that have favored the growth of a strong two-party system. Different interests and voting blocs predominate in different regions, creating a geographically

(5) fragmented electorate. This heterogeneity is complemented by a federal political structure that forces the major parties to find voter support at state and local levels in separate regions. For example, the Democratic Party long sought and drew support simultaneously from northern Black urban voters and segregationists. Such pressures encourage the major parties to avoid

(10) political programs that are too narrowly or sharply defined. The nondoctrinal character of U.S. politics means that important new issues and voting blocs tend to be initially ignored by the major parties. Such issues—opposition to immigration and the abolition of slavery are two historic examples—tend to gain political prominence through third parties.

(15) Ironically, the same factors that lead to the emergence of third parties contribute to their failure to gain national political power. Parties based on narrow or ephemeral issues remain isolated or fade rapidly. At the same time, those that raise increasingly urgent social issues also face inherent limits to growth. Long before a third party can begin to substantially broaden its base

(20) of voter support, the major parties are able to move to attract the minority of voters that it represents. The Democratic Party, for instance, appropriated the agrarian platform of the Populist Party in 1896 and enacted Socialist welfare proposals in the 1930s, in both cases winning much of the popular bases of these parties. Except for the Republican Party, which gained national

(25) prominence as the Whigs were declining in the 1850s, no third party has ever achieved national major party status. Only at state and local levels have a handful of third parties been sustained by a stable voting bloc that remains unrepresented by a major party.

8. The primary purpose of this passage is to

  ○ examine the appeal of U.S. national third parties to the electorate at state and local levels.

  ○ trace the historical rise and decline of third party movements in the United States.

  ○ explain why most U.S. third-party movements have failed to gain major party status.

  ○ demonstrate that U.S. politics has traditionally been nonideological in character.

  ○ suggest a model to explain why certain U.S. third-party movements have succeeded while others have failed.

9. Which of the following does the author suggest was an important factor in the establishment of the Republican Party as a major national party?

  ○ The polarization of national opinion at the time of a major social crisis

  ○ The unique appeal of its program to significant sectional interests

  ○ The acceptance of its program by a large bloc of voters unrepresented by a major party

  ○ The simultaneous decline of an established major party

  ○ The inability of the major parties of the era to appeal to all sectional interests

10. According to the author, the major factor responsible for the rise of third parties in the United States has been the

  ○ domination of major parties by powerful economic interests.

  ○ inability of major parties to bring about broad consensus among a variety of voters and interest groups.

  ○ slow response of major parties to new issues and voting groups.

  ○ exclusion of immigrants and minorities from the mainstream of U.S. politics.

  ○ variety of motivations held by voting blocs in different regions.

Shopping-mall developers seek to attract large department stores that will act as "anchors"—high-traffic stores that will bring many customers into the complex. However, when a department store chain seeks to site a new store, it must take into consideration that the high level of customer traffic generated

(5)  by the new store may be exploited by nearby smaller retailers. It will decline to build if it is judged that the large store's "positive externality" will serve primarily to increase sales at nearby small competitors. Mall developers can circumvent this problem and retain a mixture of large and small retailers by internalizing the department store's externality—that is, by bringing some of

(10)  the benefits associated with the department store back to the store itself.

The ability of malls to do so lies in the fact that their developers own the entire complex. They can charge rents that reflect not only the contribution that each store makes to the mall's overall revenues but also the business that a store brings to the mall's other tenants. Recent studies of malls in the

(15)  American Midwest show that in a mall with two or three department stores, a small shoe store or restaurant might pay rent per square foot that is five times the rate charged to department stores in the complex, while a jeweler in a mall with four or five department stores could pay twenty times the rate paid by the mall's anchors.

(20)  The partiality shown department stores increases with mall size, even though the study shows that department stores in different-sized complexes usually generate about the same sales per square foot. The disparity in the rents charged between department stores and small retailers cannot be explained simply by the fact that small stores make greater sales per square

(25)  foot of floor space; rather, the smaller stores are willing to subsidize the department stores for the sales that department stores generate for them, and the greater the traffic, the more they are willing to pay.

11. The author's primary purpose in writing this passage is to

    ◯ indicate the competitive advantages that malls have over traditional shopping districts.

    ◯ introduce the concept of positive externality and explain its relevance to shopping malls located in the American Midwest.

    ◯ argue that mall owners exploit small stores by manipulating their rents so that large store owners benefit.

    ◯ explain how mall developers attempt to increase customer traffic for a mall by varying rental rates for different kinds of stores.

    ◯ demonstrate how mall developers maximize the number of retailers in their malls by internalizing the benefits of positive externality.

12. Which of the following can be inferred from the passage?

    ◯ Jewelers in small malls pay more rent per square foot than do shoe stores in large malls.

    ◯ Department store chains consider more than potential sales per square foot when determining where to locate stores.

    ◯ If mall developers were to charge the same rent per square foot for every store, malls would likely experience a surplus of department stores and a shortage of smaller retailers.

    ◯ Positive externality is a greater problem for small stores than for larger department stores.

    ◯ If not for the phenomenon of positive externality, malls would not be able to attract large department stores as tenants.

13. Which of the following statements about large malls and small malls can be logically inferred from the passage?

    ○ Department stores in large malls generate more sales per square foot than do department stores in small malls.

    ○ Small malls tend to attract more specialized stores than large malls and, therefore, do not need as many anchor stores.

    ○ The disparity in rent per square foot between small retailers and anchor stores is greater in larger malls than smaller malls.

    ○ Small retailers in large malls often resent paying higher rent than anchor stores and eventually move to smaller malls where the disparity is less pronounced.

    ○ Because larger malls are normally assumed to attract an upscale clientele, they can charge small retailers more rent per square foot than smaller malls can.

    For many years, the observation that certain intensely bright young stars are concentrated along the spiral arms of disk-shaped galaxies remained unexplained. But recent research suggests both a solution to the puzzle of these "O-stars," which are a million times brighter than the sun, and a
(5)  mechanism that may partially explain the process of star formation in general.
    Astronomers have long been aware that stars are made up of interstellar gas and dust, but until recently the specific sequence of events that signaled their birth was a mystery. Today, however, the stars in spiral arms of disk-shaped galaxies are thought to result from density waves induced by gravitational
(10) fluctuations at the galactic center. These waves appear to function as the lines along which scattered clouds of interstellar gas and dust collect into much larger clouds, which then coalesce into clumps of high concentration out of which different types of stars, including O-stars, eventually emerge. Extensive mapping of these cloud complexes, or nebulas, has established a correlation
(15) between these complexes and O-stars—a coincidence too striking, in view of the expanse of empty space within galaxies, to be the result of chance.
    Since they produce a red florescence, O-stars are usually found in glowing nebulas that astronomers have labeled H II regions. O-stars cannot migrate out of these regions because their life spans are too short. Therefore, astronomers
(20) have studied H II regions to determine how clouds and O-stars interact.

These observations suggest that the interaction between clouds and O-stars is a self-perpetuating cycle in which stars will be produced until the cloud material is used up. O-stars consume their fuel rapidly and release huge amounts of energy. Moreover, O-star radiation contributes to driving
(25) a shock wave into these clouds, compressing gas and dust there. Out of this tremendous compression of gas and dust arises a second generation of young stars, among them new O-stars.

14. Which of the following best describes the organization of the passage?

○ A puzzle is presented, and then two possible scientific solutions are discussed.

○ A new phenomenon is described, and then the scientific methods used to study it are discussed.

○ Recent scientific research is described and then applied to solve an existing problem.

○ A previously known phenomenon is described and then explained by scientific observations.

○ A number of scientific hypotheses are discussed, and then observations concerning their validity are described.

15. The passage states all of the following about O-stars EXCEPT that

○ they are much bigger than the sun.

○ they are found in glowing nebulas.

○ they consume their fuel quickly.

○ they emit large amounts of radiation.

○ they cannot migrate out of H II regions.

16. According to the passage, interstellar gas and dust coalesce into "clumps of high concentration" (line 12)

    ○ only in H II regions of space.

    ○ because of gravitational fluctuations in galactic arms.

    ○ when O-stars migrate out of H II regions.

    ○ after releasing huge amounts of energy.

    ○ before new stars are formed.

17. The author mentions "O-star radiation" (line 24) in order to

    ○ explain why O-stars have short life spans.

    ○ outline the role of O-stars in star formation.

    ○ emphasize the reddish glow of certain nebulas.

    ○ prove that O-stars interact with cloud complexes.

    ○ predict the rate at which nebulas use up their gas and dust.

## THE WRAP-UP

Reading Comprehension can be just as predictable as any other section of the GMAT. Reading strategically with Kaplan's method will allow you to better understand what you read in less time, because the method is designed specifically to extract what the GMAT tests for. Keep the following in mind:

- Always read with the author's intent in mind.
- Road maps allow you to research answers quickly when necessary.
- Do not read with the goal of memorizing every last detail.

Wrong answers in Global questions tend to

- be too specific;
- be too broad;
- be too strongly worded; and/or
- misrepresent/contradict the passage.

Wrong answers in Detail questions tend to

- refer to the wrong part of the passage;
- misrepresent the passage;
- go beyond the scope; and/or
- be too strongly worded.

Wrong answers in Inference questions tend to

- misrepresent the passage;
- go beyond the scope; and/or
- be too strongly worded.

# ANSWERS AND EXPLANATIONS

## U.S. THIRD-PARTY MOVEMENTS

### 8. (C)

Here the primary purpose is fairly clearly articulated in the very first sentence of the passage: "The search for an explanation of the historically weak status of U.S. third-party movements is illuminated by examining the conditions that have favored the growth of a strong two-party system." In other words, the purpose of the passage is to explain why most U.S. third-party movements have failed to gain major party status, as **(C)** puts it.

A quick vertical scan of the verbs knocks a few answer choices out. GMAT passages are never comprehensive enough to "trace the historical rise and decline" in **(B)** or "demonstrate" anything exhaustively in **(D)**. Also, eliminate **(D)** because it doesn't mention third-party movements, the topic of this passage. Eliminate **(A)** because the passage is primarily concerned with the failure of third parties to rise above the state and local levels, not their success there. Finally, eliminate **(E)** because no "model" is given to explain the success of some third-party movements; again, the passage is about the general failure of third-party movements nationally.

### 9. (D)

This is a Detail question, so you just have to scan the passage to find where the Republican Party is mentioned, near the end of the passage. The exact line states: "Except for the Republican Party, which gained national prominence as the Whigs were declining in the 1850s, no third party has ever achieved national major party status." This allows you to infer that the party's establishment was facilitated by the "simultaneous decline of an established major party," so **(D)** is correct.

Because this is a Detail question, answers from the wrong part of the passage can be counted out, including **(C)**, an irrelevant detail from the second paragraph. **(A)** is not mentioned anywhere, and neither are **(B)** or **(E)**.

### 10. (C)

You're looking for factors to explain the rise of third parties, not their ultimate failure, so you want to research the first paragraph. There it states, "important new issues and voting blocs tend to be initially ignored by the major parties. Such issues . . . tend to gain political prominence through third parties." **(C)** is a close paraphrase of this thought and, therefore, correct.

Eliminate **(A)** because "powerful economic interests" are not mentioned. **(B)** is off base: as a general rule, major parties *are* able to bring about broad consensus. Eliminate **(D)** also: if minorities were excluded from the mainstream of U.S. politics, Black urban voters would not be a significant voting bloc of the Democratic Party. Finally, eliminate **(E)** as well, because major parties generally deal with the variety of motivations held by voting blocs in different regions successfully by avoiding narrowly defined political programs.

## SHOPPING MALL ATTRACTION

### 11. (D)

The primary purpose is set up in the first paragraph: mall developers seek department stores because they bring a lot of customers to the malls. However, to get those department stores, they have to make it worthwhile for them. The next two paragraphs explain how developers solve this problem by varying rents to compensate the department stores. Therefore, the primary purpose is concisely stated in **(D)**.

(A) and (E) state ideas that are not present in the passage—a comparison with other shopping districts is not made, and maximizing the number of retailers is not discussed. (C) is way too strongly worded and contrary to the tone of the passage: it is never suggested that small stores are exploited, and in any event, hiking rents on small stores is not the main point of the passage. (B) may be tempting, because the concept of positive externality *is* important to the passage, but it's too specific, referring only to the American Midwest. The studies of Midwestern malls are brought up only to support the author's argument.

### 12. (B)

The question provides no clues as to where to look in the passage for the answer, so you have to work from the answer choices. (B) is correct because the passage states that department store chains will decline to build in a mall if their presence will "primarily" benefit other stores. Therefore, it can't be just their own sales that concern them; they also consider the benefit they provide to other stores. (B) is also a fairly softly worded choice, which you should love to see as the answer to an Inference question.

(A) goes too far: although you *are* told that jewelers sometimes pay more per square foot than shoe stores in large malls, you can't infer that the same is true of small malls. (C) states the opposite of what the passage implies. Department stores demand lower rents per square foot to compensate for their "positive externalities," so a developer offering the same rates to all stores would have a dearth of department stores. (D) likewise contradicts the passage. Smaller stores are never said to have "positive externalities," only department stores. Even if smaller stores have that "problem," nothing in the passage implies that smaller stores suffer more from that problem than do larger ones. Finally, (E) gets it wrong because the passage never suggests that positive externality is what attracts department stores to malls. The developers want the department stores for their "positive externalities," not vice versa.

### 13. (C)

Once again, with no clue as to where the answer may be, you need to go through the choices. (C) is correct because the passage states that "the partiality [in rent] shown department stores increases with mall size," which is equivalent to saying that the disparity in rent between anchor (department) stores and small stores is greater for larger malls than smaller malls.

**(A)** is contradicted by the passage, which says that sales per square foot for department stores are about the same for large and small malls. **(B)** and **(D)** aren't suggested anywhere in the passage. **(E)** makes a claim about "upscale clientele," which is not supported by the passage: the passage only explains rental rates based on customer traffic, not on how chic the store is.

## O-STARS

### 14. (D)

The good news about "hard" science passages is that you don't actually have to understand the science to get the correct answer. This Global question asks about the organization of the passage, so after quickly reading through the passage, attack the answer choices aggressively. Paragraph 1 mentions a previously known phenomenon— the location of O-stars in the spiral arms of disk-shaped galaxies. The rest of the passage explains the why and the what of this phenomenon—why O-stars form there and what function they serve there. **(D)** sums that up nicely and is, therefore, correct.

The first part of **(A)** is okay—a "puzzle" is presented—but this choice hops the tracks when it mentions two solutions. This is one of those half-right, half-wrong choices that you should watch out for. No new phenomenon is described as **(B)** states, nor are scientific methods ever discussed. **(C)** has things backward: in the passage, the problem comes before the research. Like **(B)**, **(E)** violates the scope: the author doesn't discuss a "number of scientific hypotheses."

### 15. (A)

The only comparison made between O-stars and the sun is at the end of the first paragraph, which says that O-stars are brighter than the sun, not that they're bigger. The final paragraph contains the information in **(C)** and **(D)**—that O-stars "consume their fuel rapidly" and "release huge amounts of energy." The third paragraph mentions **(B)** and **(E)**—they're "usually found in glowing nebulas" and "cannot migrate out of H II regions." That leaves **(A)** as the one that goes unmentioned.

### 16. (E)

Because the question stem sends you back to line 12, the answer is to be found in the middle of the second paragraph. The third sentence of this paragraph explicitly states that gas and dust are concentrated into dense clumps prior to the birth of stars, which is what **(E)** says.

(A) and (C) refer to the wrong part of the passage—the third paragraph. Moreover, (C) flatly contradicts information in that paragraph. (D) also refers to the wrong part of the passage—the fourth paragraph. It also pertains to O-stars, not interstellar gas and dust. Finally, (B) gets the paragraph right but, like (C), flatly contradicts the passage.

### 17. (B)

Lines 24–25 say that O-star radiation "contributes to driving a shock wave" that compresses gas and dust in clouds. The following lines go on to say that new stars emerge out of this compressed gas and dust. That's pretty much the sum of (B).

(A) and (C) are brought up in paragraph 3, but they aren't linked to O-star radiation. (D) misrepresents the author's purpose: the author is here to *explain* how O-stars and cloud complexes interact, not to *prove* it. (E) also misrepresents the author's purpose, as there's never a prediction.

Note that most questions to "hard" science passage tend to be very specific Detail questions in which either a line reference will be provided or the wording in the question will help you to locate the relevant information in the passage. Even if you don't fully understand the passage, you can often get these questions right.

# CHAPTER 7: CRITICAL REASONING

Critical Reasoning is all about arguments—your ability to analyze them, recognize assumptions, and make deductions. To master this element of the GMAT, you'll need to be able to break down arguments and evaluate their strengths and weaknesses.

The 41-question Verbal section contains around 11 Critical Reasoning questions, which account for just over 25 percent of your Verbal subscore.

The first step toward working efficiently in this section is gaining familiarity with the questions. Let's begin by looking at the directions for a Critical Reasoning question:

> **Directions:** For each question, select the best of the answer choices given.

The stimulus for each question is a short passage whose topic can be drawn from a wide variety of subjects. A stimulus generally takes the form of an argument and, like Reading Comprehension passages, won't require any outside information for you to work with it.

Critical Reasoning contains a wide variety of question types, each of which requires you to do something different with the stimulus at hand. While some answer choices may *seem* close to the correct answer, remember that the test makers created one (and only one) of them to be correct. Incorrect choices usually distort the text, misrepresent its scope, or are the opposite of what you're looking for.

# THE STRATEGY

Arguments on the GMAT are designed with one purpose in mind—to try to convince you of something. To accomplish this goal, they must do two things: tell you *what* to believe and tell you *why* to believe it. Respectively, these two things correspond to *conclusion* and *evidence*. Before moving on to the method, let's have a closer look at these two elements using a sample Critical Reasoning stimulus:

1. A recent study has concluded that, contrary to the claims of those trying to ban cigarette advertisements altogether, cigarette ads placed on billboards and in magazines have little to no effect on the smoking habits of the smokers who view the ads. The study, which surveyed more than 20,000 smokers and solicited their reasons for continuing to smoke, found that practically no one in the survey felt that these advertisements influenced their decision to smoke.

## CONCLUSION

When working with an argument, your first goal should be to locate its conclusion—the single main point that the author is trying to make—as this is *the* most important component. The conclusion will usually have a conclusion key word—such as *thus*, *therefore*, or *so*—to help you locate it but not always. The conclusion can appear anywhere in the stimulus, though it's usually the last sentence.

The conclusion is the most important part of the argument because, for starters, *every single GMAT Critical Reasoning question that contains an argument will be asking you to do something to it!* Therefore, not only is it critical (no pun intended) for you to identify it, but you'll also need to understand both its scope and its limits (more on this later).

In the previous argument, the author's agenda (or conclusion) is to convince us that "cigarette ads placed on billboards and in magazines have little to no effect on the smoking habits of the smokers who view the ads."

The scope of the argument is also important to recognize, as correct answers in any kind of Critical Reasoning question must have a direct effect on the scope of the argument, while wrong choices tend to focus on things that do not affect the correct scope.

The scope of this conclusion is "cigarette ads placed on billboards and in magazines" and "smoking habits of smokers who view the ads." Examples of things that are *not* in this scope—likely fodder for wrong choices—might be "cigarette ads on windshield wipers," "drunk driving ads on billboards and in magazines," "people who don't smoke," and "smokers who don't view the ads."

## EVIDENCE

Because the role of evidence is to support the argument's claim, the quality of that evidence determines the strength of the argument itself. On the GMAT, the quality of the evidence will always be lacking, and it will be your job to diagnose and address it. Evidence can sometimes have a key word—such as *because*, *since*, or *for*—to help you locate it.

Take another look at the argument from earlier. The scope in the evidence is "practically no one in the survey," "these advertisements," and "their decision to smoke." Notice how this scope lines up perfectly with the conclusion (i.e., they both concern the same things; this will not be true of all GMAT arguments). While an exact match is certainly one of the necessary elements of a good argument, it is by no means the only thing necessary.

## THE METHOD

GMAT Critical Reasoning arguments have many different types of questions. The first two steps of Kaplan's method for these questions is the same:

> **Step 1: Read the question stem *first* and identify the question type.**
>
> **Step 2: Read the stimulus.**

Before we break down the remaining three steps by question type, let's discuss the first two steps.

**Step 1: Read the question stem *first* and identify the question type.** Read the question stem first because GMAT Critical Reasoning stimuli are quite flexible, and several different types of questions can be asked of the same stimulus. For that reason, you will want to know exactly what you need to do to it before you worry about its contents. Otherwise, your first read of the stimulus will be rather unfocused (as you're not looking for anything in particular), which forces you to reread the stimulus and waste time.

You might insist that if all arguments have conclusion and evidence, then you should just read for those things every time. That would work on arguments, but unfortunately, not all Critical Reasoning problems on the GMAT use arguments in their stimuli and the ones that don't will *not* have conclusion and evidence.

All right, now we're ready to look at the remaining steps for each question type.

## ASSUMPTION QUESTIONS

Assumption questions can be most easily understood if we consider the following analogy:

> One Sunday afternoon in the middle of December, a group of children are having a snowball fight in someone's backyard. One mischievous kid stuffs a piece of ice into her snowball before throwing it. Her target dodges the icy mound and the snowball strikes a neighbor's window hard enough to leave a visible crack. The window's owner is now understandably upset as the window is no longer effective at keeping out the cold. Unable to catch the culprit, he calls a repairperson.

The window is the argument and it originally served its purpose well—to keep the cold out. The mischievous kid is the test maker: she makes the once-perfect window defective in some way. *You* are the repairperson. In assumption questions, it is your job to repair the window.

If you were fixing a window, you would need to examine it, pinpoint the problem, and then figure out how to fix it. On GMAT arguments, use the following method.

### Kaplan's 5-Step Method for Assumption Questions

**Step 1: Read the question stem *first* and identify the question type.**

**Step 2: Read the stimulus.**

**Step 3: Identify conclusion and evidence.**

**Step 4: Determine the weakness in the evidence.**

**Step 5: Prephrase an answer, focusing on what would repair the argument by addressing the weakness. Choose the answer choice that matches your prephrase.**

Let's apply this method to the following argument.

**Step 1: Read the question stem *first* and identify the question type.**

**Step 2: Read the stimulus.**

1. A recent study has concluded that, contrary to the claims of those trying to ban cigarette advertisements altogether, cigarette ads placed on billboards and in magazines have little to no effect on the smoking habits of the smokers who view the ads. The study, which surveyed more than 20,000 smokers and solicited their reasons for continuing to smoke, found that practically no one in the survey felt that these advertisements influenced their decision to smoke.

   The study's conclusion is based upon which of the following assumptions?

   ○ People do not switch cigarette brands based on their exposure to cigarette ads on billboards and in magazines.

   ○ Cigarette ads on billboards and in magazines do not encourage nonsmokers to take up the habit.

   ○ Banning cigarette advertisements altogether will encourage people to give up smoking.

   ○ People are consciously aware of all the reasons they choose to smoke.

   ○ People who decide to smoke do so for rational reasons.

**Step 3: Identify conclusion and evidence.** Our argument boils down to this:

*Cigarette ads placed on billboards and in magazines have little to no effect on the smoking habits of the smokers who view the ads **because** practically no one [out of more than 20,000] in the survey felt that these advertisements influenced their decision to smoke.*

Scope for conclusion and evidence is as follows:

**Conclusion:** "cigarette ads placed on billboards and in magazines" and "smoking habits of smokers who view the ads"

**Evidence:** "practically no one in the survey," "these advertisements," and "their decision to smoke"

**Step 4: Determine the weakness in the evidence.** Let's examine the evidence closely to determine the exact reason it falls short.

"Practically no one in the survey" out of more than 20,000 seems pretty convincing for a sample, "these advertisements" refer to the correct ads, and "influenced their decision to smoke" certainly supports the effect on smoking habits mentioned in the conclusion. That doesn't leave much if you ruled out everything mentioned from the given evidence. You're left with two words—"felt that." *That* has no meaning on its own, so the weakness in the evidence must come from the word *felt,* and it does—the evidence says people didn't *feel* the ads influenced them, while the conclusion claims that the ads in fact *had* little to no effect. This is a small difference, to be sure, but such is the nuance that assumption questions test.

**Step 5: Prephrase an answer, focusing on what would repair the argument by addressing the weakness. Choose the answer choice that matches your prephrase.** To patch up this little discrepancy, we'll need something like, "People always feel it whenever something influences their decision to smoke." That's pretty much what **(D)** says. Let's see why the wrong choices fall short.

**(A):** Switching brands does not affect anything on the scope list. You might be tempted to connect this to "their decision to smoke" but that's a "yes/no" issue, not a "which brand" one.

**(B):** We're not concerned with nonsmokers. The only two groups of people on our scope list are "smokers who view the ads" and the over 20,000 folks in the survey. People outside of these groups are of no consequence to the argument. (Sounds cold, but that's how arguments work.)

**(C):** This one addresses all of the correct scopes. Unfortunately, it goes completely counter to the conclusion that the ads have no effect. Valid assumptions need to *support* the conclusion.

**(E):** Rational reasons do not affect anything on our scope list, so eliminate this. (Remove it from the choice, and you don't even have a complete thought left.)

The answer is **(D)**.

**Remember:** A valid assumption needs to *fix* the problem with the argument. To do so, it must have the right direct effect on the argument's specific scopes.

## STRENGTHEN/WEAKEN QUESTIONS

Perhaps the most common type of Critical Reasoning question on the GMAT, strengthening or weakening an argument involves making its conclusion more or less likely to be true. While correct answers certainly can, they don't need to (and often don't) go all the way: a strengthener does not need to fix the argument to the degree that an assumption would, and a weakener does not need to do irreparable damage to it.

In our window example, a strengthener would be akin to taping a piece of cardboard over the crack. The newly reinforced window would block out the cold better but not necessarily quite as well as a properly repaired window. A weakener would enlarge the crack but not necessarily to the point where the window was totally useless. Let's have a look at the method.

### Kaplan's 5-Step Method for Strengthen/Weaken Questions

> **Step 1:** Read the question stem *first* and identify the question type (strengthen or weaken).
>
> **Step 2:** Read the stimulus.
>
> **Step 3:** Identify conclusion and evidence.
>
> **Step 4:** Determine the weakness in the evidence.
>
> **Step 5:** Prephrase an answer. Choose the answer choice that matches your prephrase.

For strengthen questions, focus on what would make the weakness less of an issue.

For weaken questions, focus on what would make the weakness more of an issue.

Apply this method to the following argument.

**Step 1: Read the question stem *first* and identify the question type (strengthen or weaken).**

**Step 2: Read the stimulus.**

2. Whitley Hospital's much-publicized increase in emergency room efficiency, which its spokespeople credit to new procedures for handling trauma patients, does not withstand careful analysis. The average time before treatment for all patients is nearly 40 minutes—the highest in the city. In addition, for trauma victims, who are the specific target of the guidelines, the situation is even worse: the average time before treatment is nearly half an hour—more than twice the city average.

Which of the following, if true, would most seriously weaken the conclusion about the value of the new procedures?

○ The city hospitals with the most efficient emergency rooms utilize the same procedures for handling trauma patients as does Whitley Hospital.

○ After the new procedures went into effect, Whitley's average time before treatment for trauma patients and patients in general dropped by nearly 35 percent.

○ Because trauma patients account for a large percentage of emergency room patients, procedures that hasten their treatment will likely increase overall emergency room efficiency.

○ Due to differences in location and size of staff, not all emergency rooms can be expected to reach similar levels of efficiency.

○ The recently hired administrators who instituted the new procedures also increased Whitley's emergency room staff by nearly 15 percent.

**Step 3: Identify conclusion and evidence.** The argument boils down to this:

*Whitley Hospital's emergency room efficiency did not increase **because** (1) average time before treatment for all patients is nearly 40 minutes **and** (2) average time before treatment for trauma patients is nearly half an hour—more than twice the city average.*

Scope for conclusion and evidence is as follows:

**Conclusion:** "Whitley Hospital's emergency room efficiency" and "did not increase"

**Evidence:** "average time before treatment for all patients," "nearly 40 minutes," "average time before treatment for trauma patients," and "nearly half an hour—more than twice the city average"

**Step 4: Determine the weakness in the evidence.** Let's examine the evidence closely to determine the exact reason it falls short.

The "average time before treatment" statements do indeed address "Whitley Hospital's emergency room efficiency." However, you may have noticed that "did not increase" from the conclusion is not supported in the evidence. We do have "nearly 40 minutes" and "nearly half an hour—more than twice the city average," but that only proves that Whitley's is currently *slow*. Unless we know how that compares to its previous efficiency, we won't know if the conclusion is true.

**Step 5: Prephrase an answer. Choose the answer choice that matches your prephrase.** To weaken this argument, we'll need a choice that says, "Whitley Hospital is more efficient now than it used to be," as **(B)** does. **(C)** and **(D)** seem to mention increasing efficiency in passing but they don't even mention Whitley Hospital, much less it's past efficiency. **(A)** and **(E)** make no mention of increasing efficiency at all.

The answer is **(B)**.

**Remember:** Taking a moment first to locate the argument's weakness in strengthen/weaken questions will make it a lot easier to predict what the correct answer must do.

## FLAW QUESTIONS

One of the least common question types on the GMAT involves identifying the flaw in arguments. While the correct answer in an assumption question fixes an argument and in a strengthen/weaken question makes it better or worse, it is enough simply to spot the wrong in the argument when dealing with flaw—you do not need to *do* anything to it.

In our window example, the crack on the glass is the flaw in the argument. Let's look at the method.

### Kaplan's 5-Step Method for Flaw Questions

**Step 1: Read the question stem *first* and identify the question type.**

**Step 2: Read the stimulus.**

**Step 3: Identify conclusion and evidence.**

**Step 4: Determine the weakness in the evidence.**

**Step 5: Prephrase an answer, focusing on a description of the weakness. Choose the answer choice that matches your prephrase.**

Apply this method to the following argument.

**Step 1: Read the question stem *first* and identify the question type.**

**Step 2: Read the stimulus.**

3. It doesn't surprise me that the critic on our local radio station went off on another tirade today about the city men's choir, as it's not the first time. Nevertheless this time, his criticisms were simply inaccurate and unjustified. For ten minutes, he spoke of nothing but the choir's lack of expressiveness. As a professional vocal instructor, I have met with these singers individually; I can state with complete confidence that each of the members of the choir has quite an expressive voice.

Which one of the following is the most serious flaw in the author's reasoning?

- He directs his argument against the critic's character rather than against his claims.

- He ignores evidence that the critic's remarks might in fact be justified.

- He cites his own professional expertise as the sole explanation for his defense of the choir.

- He assumes that a group will have a given attribute if each of its parts has that attribute.

- He attempts to conclude the truth of a general situation from evidence about one specific situation.

**Step 3: Identify conclusion and evidence.** The argument boils down to this:

> *The city men's choir does not lack expressiveness **because** I, a professional vocal instructor, met with each singer individually and can vouch for his expressiveness.*

Scope for conclusion and evidence is as follows:

**Conclusion:** "The city men's choir" and "not lack expressiveness"

**Evidence:** "Professional vocal instructor," "each singer individually," and "can vouch for his expressiveness"

**Step 4: Determine the weakness in the evidence.** Let's examine the evidence closely to determine the exact reason it falls short.

"Professional vocal instructor" and ""can vouch for his expressiveness" would certainly support "not lack expressiveness." However, "each singer individually" does not quite prove "the city men's choir"—what's true of a part is not necessarily true of the whole.

**Step 5: Prephrase an answer, focusing on a description of the weakness. Choose the answer choice that matches your prephrase. (D)** is an exact match for our prediction. Each of the wrong choices in a flaw question will include at least one specific thing that the author did not do. The argument against the critic's character, the ignored evidence, and the general situation from **(A)**, **(B)**, and **(E)**, respectively, do not exist in the passage. While the author *does* cite his professional expertise, that is not the "sole explanation" for his defense, since he also met with the singers and checked them out firsthand, so **(C)** is out as well.

The answer is **(D)**.

**Remember:** Flaw questions only want to you *describe* the flaw in the argument.

## INFERENCE QUESTIONS

The remaining two Critical Reasoning question types on the GMAT do not deal with arguments. As such, you will not be locating conclusion and evidence for either. The first of these two is Inference, and you are likely to see one or two of these on Test Day.

Inference question stimuli present a passage full of factual statements. Their question stems tend to ask for what *must be true*, *is most strongly supported*, *is implied*, or *can be inferred*. While the wording on these sounds rather weak, don't be fooled—in Inference, you are **always** looking for the choice that absolutely cannot be false if the statements in the stimulus are true. For that reason, a great way to test the choices to an Inference question is simply to evaluate the possible truth of the *opposite* of each choice. What must be true by definition cannot be false, so the choice whose opposite would contradict the passage is the inference that you need. Let's have a look at the method.

### Kaplan's 5-Step Method for Inference Questions

**Step 1: Read the question stem *first* and identify the question type.**

**Step 2: Read the stimulus.**

**Step 3: Identify the individual statements in the passage.**

**Step 4: Combine the given statements to form a deduction.**

**Step 5: If no deduction is apparent, look for the choice whose opposite would contradict the stimulus.**

Let's apply this to the following question.

**Step 1: Read the question stem *first* and identify the question type.**

**Step 2: Read the stimulus.**

4. When parents allow their children to spend a large amount of time watching television, those children see many more images of violence than do children who watch very little television. The more violent images a child sees, the more violent that child will become. The more violent a child is, the more likely the child is to commit crimes as an adult.

   If the statements in the passage above are true, which of the following must also be true?

   ○ With an increase in the number of acts of violence committed by children, one can expect to find a concurrent increase in the amount of television watched by children.

   ○ If parents did not allow their children to watch television, juvenile delinquency would be unlikely.

○ No child will develop an aversion to violence if he or she is permitted to watch television.

○ The more parents try to discourage their children from watching television, the more likely those children are to become criminals.

○ If a child sees more images of violence on television, the likelihood of that child committing crimes as an adult increases.

**Step 3: Identify the individual statements in the passage.** Our statements boil down to these:

1. The more TV kids are allowed to watch, the more violent imagery they are exposed to.

2. The more violent imagery they are exposed to, the more violent they become.

3. The more violent they become, the more likely they will be to commit crimes as adults.

**Step 4: Combine the given statements to form a deduction.** So basically, children who watch a lot of TV are more likely to grow up as criminals. That matches **(E)** perfectly.

**Step 5: If no deduction is apparent, look for the choice whose opposite would contradict the stimulus**. If you did not notice the deduction that children who watch a lot of TV are more likely to grow up as criminals as you read the stimulus, you will need to test each choice to see if it *must be true*. (Only do this if step 4 doesn't yield a deduction!)

Here's how that would work:

**(A)**: Based on the stimulus, is it possible for there to be an increase in the number of acts of violence committed by children but *not* a concurrent increase in the amount of TV they watch? Sure, while TV is presented as *one way* to violence, nowhere in the stimulus does it claim to be the *only* way. You might not know if this negated statement is true, but its truth certainly does not directly contradict anything in the stimulus, so it does not have to be true.

**(B):** Based on the stimulus, is it possible for juvenile delinquency to be *likely* despite parents not allowing their kids to watch TV? There is no direct contradiction here to the original (as we have nothing on juvenile delinquency), so this choice doesn't need to be true either.

**(C):** Based on the stimulus, is it possible for *at least one* child to develop an aversion to violence when allowed to watch TV? Of course: aversion to violence is never even discussed, so this cannot possibly contradict anything in the stimulus. Therefore, this choice doesn't need to be true.

**(D):** Based on the stimulus, is it possible that the more parents discourage TV watching, the *less* likely the kids become criminals? Instead of contradicting, the negation of this choice would actually be true. That makes **(D)** the opposite of what we are looking for.

Let's see what happens if you try negating the correct choice:

**(E):** Based on the stimulus, is it possible that the more violence a kid sees on TV, the *less* likely that kid is to commit crimes as an adult? There is no way for this negation to be true, as it directly contradicts our statements.

**Remember:** Wrong answer choices in Inference questions usually step beyond the scope of the stimulus. If you don't have enough information to judge something either way, it is not an inference.

## EXPLAIN QUESTIONS

The last type of Critical Reasoning question is the Explain question. Like Inference, Explain questions also do not feature an argument. Instead, the stimulus to an Explain question will contain two or more *seemingly* contradictory facts. Your job is to explain why there is, in fact, no contradiction. You should expect to see at least one Explain question on Test Day. Let's look at the method.

### Kaplan's 5-Step Method for Explain Questions

**Step 1: Read the question stem.**

**Step 2: Read the stimulus.**

**Step 3: Locate the contradictory elements.**

**Step 4: Try to explain how these elements can coexist.**

**Step 5: Look for the choice that addresses *both* sides of the contradiction.**

Let's apply this to the following question.

**Step 1: Read the question stem.**

**Step 2: Read the stimulus.**

5. The number of applicants applying to top graduate programs has declined by more than 10 percent since the mid-1990s. Nonetheless, the number of students admitted to these same programs has not decreased appreciably, and the caliber of the students admitted, as measured by their undergraduate GPAs and standardized test scores, has actually improved markedly.

   Which of the following, if true, best explains the seemingly contradictory trends described above?

   ○ The number of applicants applying to second- and third-tier graduate programs has also declined by more than 10 percent since the mid-1990s.

   ○ Many potential graduate school applicants are put off by the ever-increasing cost of a graduate education.

   ○ The higher premium offered to the graduates of top graduate programs has made the applicant pool increasingly competitive, discouraging those with lower GPAs or standardized test scores from applying.

   ○ Because of improved economic opportunities, particularly in Internet start-up companies and other high-tech industries, general interest in leaving the workforce to go to graduate school has waned in recent years.

   ○ The number of women applying to top graduate programs has increased since the mid-1990s, while at the same time, the number of men applying to top graduate programs has declined.

**Step 3: Locate the contradictory elements.** The confusion here comes from the fact that *fewer* people are applying to top graduate programs yet the programs are still accepting about the same number of students and these students are actually *better* than the usual crop.

Much as in assumption questions, the answer to an Explain question must directly affect the scope of the problem. Let's identify the scopes of the contradictory elements:

1. "number of applicants applying to top graduate programs" and "declined by more than 10 percent since the mid-1990s"

2. "number of students admitted to these programs," "not decreased appreciably," and "caliber of students admitted has improved markedly"

**Step 4: Try to explain how these elements can coexist.** To explain this mystery, the correct choice will need to stay within the scopes defined and answer how *fewer* applicants to top graduate programs could actually result in a *higher* caliber of student.

**Step 5: Look for the choice that addresses *both* sides of the contradiction.** (C) resolves the mystery perfectly: if the lesser students have been discouraged from even applying, that would explain why fewer applicants in the pool does not necessarily force schools to lower standards. Let's see where the wrong choices go wrong:

**(A):** This choice focuses on "second- and third-tier graduate programs," which is not within the scope of our question.

**(B):** This one explains why the applicant pool is getting smaller, but it does nothing to explain why the student caliber is rising.

**(D):** As with **(B)**, this choice also explains why the pool is getting smaller but does nothing to explain why student caliber is on the rise.

**(E):** Men versus women is completely irrelevant to either issue.

**Remember:** To explain a mystery, the correct choice must address *both* halves of that mystery. Common wrong choices in Explain questions deepen the mystery, explain only one half, make an irrelevant comparison, or step beyond the scope of the question.

Now it's your turn!

# PRACTICE SET

6. Advertisement: Quicktrak is gaining more subscribers each year than any other business news service. Quicktrak offers the most up-to-date international business news and the most comprehensive company information needed to make wise investment decisions. Quicktrak is the only service devoted exclusively to international business news and the financial analysis of corporations. So by choosing a financial news service other than Quicktrak, you are doing your company a disservice.

   Which of the following is an assumption of the argument in the advertisement above?

   ○ A subscription to Quicktrak is not appreciably more expensive than a subscription to standard business magazines or newspapers.

   ○ A significant portion of any company's business involves international trade or investing in other companies.

   ○ Quicktrak has more subscribers than other business news services.

   ○ The market share of Quicktrak is increasing.

   ○ Choosing a financial news service other than Quicktrak is worse than choosing no financial news service at all.

7. Enrollment in graduate and professional programs tends to be high in a strong economy and much lower during recessions. The perceived likelihood of future job availability, therefore, affects people's willingness to pass up immediate earning potential to invest in career-related training.

   This argument assumes that

   ○ the perceived likelihood of job availability has decreased in recent years.

   ○ all those who avoid graduate and professional school during an economic slump do so because of the perceived lack of future jobs.

   ○ perceptions of the likelihood of job availability are related to the state of the economy.

   ○ those who enroll in graduate and professional schools during a strong economy help increase the economy's strength.

   ○ graduate and professional programs admit fewer students during recessions.

8. Staff members at the Willard Detention Center typically oversee students' schedules and make all final decisions regarding the required activities in which students participate. Students are permitted, however, to make their own decisions regarding how they spend their free time. Therefore, students should be permitted to make their own decisions regarding the elective courses that they wish to take.

This conclusion would be more reasonably drawn if which of the following were inserted into the argument as an additional premise?

- ◯ Decisions regarding required activities are more important than decisions regarding the elective courses that students take.
- ◯ Students are more willing to take elective courses than to participate in required Center activities.
- ◯ Required activities contribute more to the students' rehabilitation than do their free-time activities.
- ◯ Staff members at Willard have found that elective courses are more beneficial for students than the available free-time activities.
- ◯ When compared for decision-making purposes, elective courses are more like free-time activities than required activities.

9. **The university's decision to scale back significantly its teaching of the literary and philosophical classics of the Western tradition is misguided.** Proponents of the move argue that today's students are not interested in these works and desire more practical, business-related courses that will help them in their future careers. But any student lacking a sufficient grounding in the thought and tradition that underlie the present civilization cannot be said to be fully educated. **The classics are the primary vehicle for instilling such knowledge.**

Which of the following best expresses the relationship between the two bolded statements above?

- ◯ The first statement offers a hypothesis, and the second statement offers conflicting evidence.
- ◯ The first statement suggests an alternative explanation for the phenomenon described in the second statement.

○ The second statement provides evidence for a conclusion drawn in the first statement.

○ The second statement must be true for the first statement to be true.

○ The second statement is an inference drawn from the first statement.

10. The average math score on a statewide proficiency exam for students attending Middlebury High School last year was 20 points higher than the average math score for students attending nearby Ellingsford High School. Therefore, any student at Ellingsford High School wishing to achieve a better math score on next September's proficiency exam should transfer to Middlebury High School over the summer.

Which of the following statements, if true, would most significantly strengthen the conclusion drawn in the passage?

○ One-third of all the students who have transferred to Middlebury High School the summer before taking the test got scores that were at least 20 points higher than the average score at Ellingsford High School.

○ Middlebury High School students who transfer to Ellingsford High School in the summer before they take the proficiency exam get average scores that are comparable to the average scores of students who remain at Middlebury.

○ Middlebury High School offers its students a unique, weeklong course just before they take the proficiency exam that has consistently proven effective in raising student scores.

○ In the past five years, the average score at Ellingsford High School has been rising at a faster rate than has the average score at Middlebury High School.

○ Students wanting better proficiency-exam scores are transferring to Middlebury High School at a high rate, which will ultimately result in a lowering of the school's average score.

11. A study found that last year, roughly 6,000 homeless people in the United States were admitted to hospitals due to malnutrition. In the same year, a little more than 10,000 nonhomeless people were admitted to hospitals for the same reason. These findings clearly show that the nonhomeless are more likely to suffer from malnutrition than are the homeless.

    The answer to which of the following questions would be most likely to point out the illogical nature of the conclusion drawn above?

    ◯ What is the relative level of severity of the malnutrition suffered by each group cited in the study?

    ◯ To what extent, on average, are the nonhomeless better off financially than are the homeless?

    ◯ To what extent are the causes of malnutrition in the nonhomeless related to ignorance of proper dietary habits?

    ◯ What percentage of each group cited in the study suffered from malnutrition last year?

    ◯ What effect would a large increase in the number of homeless shelters have on the incidence of malnutrition among the homeless?

12. History has shown that severe and sudden political instability strikes Country X roughly once every 50 years. The most recent example was the attempt on the president's life in 1992. The reaction of average investors in Country X to crisis situations in the country cannot be predicted in advance. The government's fiscal affairs department has introduced an electronic protection mechanism into the market in the hopes of avoiding a prolonged, large-scale sell-off. The mechanism is triggered in specific instances based on estimations of how average investors will react to changes in corporate data and economic indicators.

    If the statements above are true, which of the following conclusions can be drawn regarding the electronic protection mechanism?

    ◯ Sometime within the next 50 years, severe and sudden political instability in Country X will trigger the protection mechanism.

    ◯ Whether the protection mechanism will function appropriately in response to a sudden political event depends on whether the event is seen by investors as positive or negative.

○ It is unclear how well the protection mechanism would work in the event of a sudden political coup if such an event is partially or wholly unrelated to changes in corporate data and economic indicators.

○ There would be no way for the protection mechanism to differentiate between market fluctuations resulting from economic factors and those that are caused by political instability.

○ The protection mechanism would be purposely destroyed by political insurgents if they were able to infiltrate the government's fiscal affairs department.

13. Country X complains that Country Y's high tariffs on imported goods have artificially inflated the price of cars imported from Country X into Country Y and that this is the reason that few of Country X's cars are sold in Country Y. On the other hand, Country X's very low tariffs allow Country Y to sell many cars there at relatively low prices. Country X says that if Country Y would lower its tariffs, then Country X's cars would be able to compete in Country Y and an equitable balance of trade would be achieved.

Which of the following, if true, would most undermine the validity of Country X's explanation for the poor sales of its cars in Country Y?

○ In places where the tariffs on goods from both countries are equal, Country Y's cars far outsell cars from Country X.

○ Cars imported from Country Z sell poorly in Country Y.

○ In countries where tariffs on imported goods are higher than in Country Y, Country X sells more cars than does Country Y.

○ Other goods from Country X sell poorly in Country Y.

○ Sales of Country Y's cars are high even in countries that have higher tariffs on imported goods than does Country X.

14. Due to a string of dismal performances, a touring band has begun to lose its audience. News of the disappointing concerts has traveled quickly via cable stations and the Internet and has negatively influenced ticket sales for future performances. Due to the poor ticket sales, a number of promoters have canceled the band's upcoming shows, forcing the band to attempt to recoup its touring and recording expenses from fewer total performances.

Which of the following, if true, taken together with the information given, best supports the prediction that more of the band's shows will be canceled?

- ◯ The promoters who canceled shows did so with the promise that they would monitor the band's reception in other cities before deciding whether or not to reschedule the canceled shows.

- ◯ The pressure to restore its diminishing fan base and recoup its overall expenses from a decreased number of performing opportunities is likely to cause the band to perform poorly in future concerts.

- ◯ Because of the canceled shows, it will be impossible for the band to earn a profit on the current tour.

- ◯ If the band cannot salvage the tour, its next CD will likely fail economically unless the band can restore its image through music videos.

- ◯ It is impossible for the management of a rock band to predict accurately the success of a tour, because fans of rock bands are notoriously fickle in their tastes.

15. Many adults, no matter what their age, respond to adversity by seeking advice only from their parents. Consciously or not, they regress to a psychological state of childhood dependence in which the parent is seen as the only source of wisdom and comfort. Adults who do not regress to this childhood mode turn for advice in adversity only to other loved ones—a spouse or a best friend—whom they perceive and relate to as peers.

If all of the statements given in the argument are true, which of the following must also be true?

- One's parents offer more wisdom in adversity than those whom one perceives as peers.
- Adults who do not suffer adversity look only to their parents for advice.
- No adults seek advice in adversity from total strangers.
- Adults who seek advice in adversity from their parents do not expect to receive wisdom and comfort.
- Adults who regress to a state of childhood dependence lose touch with their peers.

## THE WRAP-UP

The key to mastering the Critical Reasoning section on the GMAT is in knowing how to approach these questions methodically. As we've seen, that means efficiently extracting what you need from the stimulus and leaving the junk behind. Keep the following in mind:

- Focusing on an argument's conclusion and evidence makes the argument a lot easier to grasp.
- Stimuli that do not feature arguments tend not to have a conclusion.

# ANSWERS AND EXPLANATIONS

## 6. (B)

The argument claims that you'd be doing your company a disservice if you choose a financial news service other than Quicktrak. You should believe that because according to the stimulus, Quicktrak is the only service devoted exclusively to the most up-to-date international business and the most comprehensive company information needed to make wise investment decisions. Now you might be thinking to yourself, "That's great if I actually care about those two things," and you'd be right! For this claim to hold, it must be true that every company out there would need those things, and that's what **(B)** gets at.

**(A)**, **(C)**, and **(E)** all contain irrelevant comparisons. **(D)** is certainly good news for Quicktrak, but it provides no reason for companies to need its service.

## 7. (C)

The argument uses an observation that more people seem to go back to school in a strong economy than in a weak one to claim that perception of job availability affects people's decision to go back to school. Well, that's not much different from saying, "I wore a blue hat this morning and got to work late, so the blue hat must have been the reason for my tardiness." For this argument to work, perception of job availability must be related to the strength of the economy—that is, this isn't simply a coincidence—so the author must be assuming **(C)**.

**(A)** mentions the job perception, but it does not address the economy. **(B)** and **(D)** go outside of scope. You're not concerned with people who *avoid* school, only those who do go back, and you are certainly not concerned with "increas[ing] the economy's strength." **(E)** simply restates part of the evidence and, therefore, adds nothing to the argument itself.

## 8. (E)

"Students should be permitted to make their own decisions regarding … elective courses," the argument says. You should we believe that because…well, all you know is that the staff has final say on required activities while students get to decide how to spend their own free time. Because that's all the evidence you have, the author must be assuming **(E)**—that elective courses are more like free time than required activities.

Each of the wrong choices features an irrelevant comparison. "Importance," "willingness," "contribution to rehabilitation," and "benefit," while important to the detention staff, are of no consequence to the argument itself.

### 9. (C)

Bolded statement questions such as this one will simply ask for the relationship between the two bolded statements, so there isn't really a method you need to follow other than to read the statements and figure out how they relate. As with any other problem that features an argument, your first step should be to find the conclusion and evidence.

In this argument, the first sentence happens to be the conclusion. That fact alone allows you to eliminate **(B)**, **(D)**, and **(E)**. To find the correct answer, all you need to do is to check if the second statement offers conflicting evidence. It does not, so **(C)** is correct.

### 10. (C)

The argument claims that Middlebury students seem to test better than Ellingsford students, so ambitious Ellingsford students should transfer if they want to do better. Well, that assumes a lot of things, one of which being that Middlebury is actually offering its students some sort of edge on this test. If it's just a coincidence or if Middlebury students just happen to be better in math, then transferring would do no good. To strengthen this argument, it needs to be true that just being with Middlebury gives you some kind of edge on this test, and that's **(C)**.

**(A)** is tricky, but knowing that a third of the transfers did better than those who stayed doesn't help. For all you know, the other two-thirds of the transfers could've ended up doing worse than those who stayed. **(B)** would actually weaken the argument. If a student from Middlebury transfers to Ellingsford and still scores well, it lessens the chance that being with Middlebury is the reason for high scores. **(D)** presents an irrelevant comparison. Ellingsford's math scoring prowess could be shooting through the roof, but that doesn't address whether its students could do better by transferring. **(E)**'s "high rate" of transfer and its ultimate "lowering of the school's average score" are also irrelevant.

## 11. (D)

"People who aren't homeless are *more* likely to suffer from malnutrition than are homeless folks!" It's true and there's proof—roughly 6,000 homeless were admitted to hospitals for malnutrition compared to over 10,000 nonhomeless folks admitted for the same reason. If you've been following the Kaplan method, however, you might have noticed the one weakness in the conclusion—the phrase "more likely." Likeliness is a function of percentage, not of absolute numbers, so knowing the *number* of people admitted for malnutrition tells you that you need the *percentage* that each number represents to judge this argument, and that's (D).

Each of the wrong choices focuses on irrelevant issues.

## 12. (C)

The stem alerts you to the existence of an "electronic protection mechanism," and you're asked to draw a conclusion about it. So what do you know about this mechanism? You know that the government introduced it to avoid "a prolonged large-scale sell-off" and that it triggers "in specific instances based on estimations of how average investors will react to changes in corporate data and economic indicators." Basically, if the corporate data and economic indicators do their thing, this mechanism will go off. If they *don't*, however, you don't actually have any information on what would happen. The latter deduction is (C).

There's no way to know whether the mechanism will trigger in the next 50 years as (A) states, because triggering depends on corporate data and economic indicators. (B)'s "investor perception," (D)'s "differentiation," and (E)'s "purposeful destruction" step beyond the scope of the question.

## 13. (A)

The argument develops from evidence that Y's high tariffs make X's cars relatively expensive but X's low tariffs make Y's cars relatively cheap. The argument concludes that if Y lowered its tariffs, then real competition and an equitable balance of trade would result. Country X basically assumes that it's doing so poorly because of the price difference created by the different tariffs. To weaken the argument, you'll need another reason for X's poor market performance. (A) achieves this by showing how Y's cars are still outselling X's where there is a level playing field. This implies that something other than tariffs—the reason offered by X for its poor performance in the car market—could very well explain the difference in sales. (Maybe X just produces lousy cars).

(**B**) does not rule out high tariffs as the culprit. (**C**), if anything, strengthens the argument. On a more level playing field in which cars from X and Y are presumably subject to the same tariffs, X's cars do better than Y's. This suggests that X may be right in stating that the high tariff is responsible for its poor sales in Country Y. (**D**) presents no problem for the explanation, because the tariffs may exist for other goods as well. (**E**) offers information that gives you no basis for comparing X's car sales with Y's car sales. You don't know, for example, how X's cars do in these countries, so this information has no real effect on the claim in the stimulus.

### 14. (B)

Dismal performances led to a drop in ticket sales for future concerts, which in turn led concert promoters to cancel concerts, putting additional pressure on the band to make up the lost money from fewer shows. You're looking for the choice that leads to more canceled shows, and it's not easy to predict the answer here. Nevertheless, you can test each choice to see where it fits into this chain of events, if at all. Canceled concerts must now lead to a result that will trigger additional canceled concerts. You already know what has led to canceled concerts: dismal performances and lower ticket sales. (**B**) mentions the former—spiraling losses will lead to even poorer performance. With (**B**) true, you would expect more canceled shows on the horizon.

(**A**)'s "promoter promise of possible rescheduling," (**C**)'s "profit," (**D**)'s "CD prospects," and (**E**)'s "management prediction" have nothing to do with cancelling more shows.

### 15. (C)

Reading the passage, you learn that adults can be divided into two groups: adults who seek advice in adversity only from their parents and the remainder, who seek that advice only from other loved ones. There is not much room here for argument. All adults fall into one or the other of these categories but not both. If these statements are true, then adults must turn either to parents or to other loved ones in times of adversity and to no one else. (**C**) is a valid inference, given the evidence above. Adults seek advice from parents or other loved ones—not from strangers. If some adults seek advice in adversity from total strangers, then the evidence has been contradicted.

(A) makes an irrelevant comparison between things that we have no information on. (B)'s "adults who do not suffer adversity," (D)'s "expect to receive wisdom and comfort," and (E)'s "lose touch with their peers" are all outside of the scope.

# Part Three

# GMAT RESOURCES

# APPENDIX 1: GRAMMAR REFERENCE GUIDE

## SENTENCE STRUCTURE

Understanding the basic rules of sentence structure enables you to spot the classic GMAT errors quickly. The fundamental principles described here will play a role in nearly every Sentence Correction item you see, whether in the original version or among some of the answer choices. Especially if English is not your native language, be sure to know this basic material.

### RUN-ON SENTENCES

When a sentence consists of more than one clause (a group of words that contains a subject and a verb), those clauses must be joined properly. It is never acceptable to hook two clauses together with a comma, as the "sentence" below does. That's called a run-on sentence.

**Wrong:** Nietzsche moved to Basel in 1869, he planned to teach classical philology.

There are a number of acceptable ways to fix a run-on.

**Correct:** Nietzsche moved to Basel in 1869; he planned to teach classical philology.

**Also Correct:** Nietzsche planned to teach classical philology; therefore, he moved to Basel in 1869.

**Also Correct:** Nietzsche moved to Basel in 1869, and he planned to teach classical philology. (The word *and*, like *or*, *for*, *but*, *nor*, and *yet*, is what's called a *coordinating conjunction*.)

**Also Correct:** Because Nietzsche planned to teach classical philology, he moved to Basel in 1869. (The word *because*, like *although, if, though,* etc., is what's called a *subordinating conjunction.*)

**Also Correct:** Nietzsche, who planned to teach classical philology, moved to Basel in 1869. (The word *who*, like *which, where, whom, that,* and *whose*, is what's called a *relative pronoun.*)

## SENTENCE FRAGMENTS

Every sentence must contain at least one complete independent clause. If there is no independent clause at all, or if what's supposed to be the independent clause is incomplete, you've got a sentence fragment.

**Wrong:** While most people, who have worked hard for many years, have not managed to save any money, although they are trying to be more frugal now.

This sentence fragment consists of nothing but subordinate clauses. One of the subordinate clauses must be made into an independent clause.

**Correct:** Most people, who have worked hard for many years, have not managed to save any money, although they are trying to be more frugal now.

**Also Correct:** While most people, who have worked hard for many years, have not managed to save any money, they are trying to be more frugal now.

# SUBJECT-VERB AGREEMENT

Remember, in English, a subject and its verb must agree in number and person. Number refers to whether a subject (or a verb) is singular or plural. Person refers to first person (*I, we*), second person (*you*), and third person (*he, she, it, one, they*).

## INTERVENING PHRASES

When the subject of a sentence is followed by a phrase (a group of words that does not have a subject and verb) or relative clause, the words are not part of the subject. They simply add information about that subject.

Learn to recognize groups of words that can come between the subject and verb!

1.  Relative clauses, which contain important information about the subject of another clause, are very often placed between a subject and verb. (The previous sentence contains a relative clause.)

    **Wrong:**        John Clare, *who during the mid-nineteenth century wrote many fine poems on rural themes*, were confined for decades to an insane asylum.

The subject is *John Clare*, which is singular, but the verb is *were*, which is plural. The fact that the relative clause ends with a plural noun (*themes*) is supposed to distract you from the fact that the subject and verb don't agree.

    **Correct:**      John Clare, who during the mid-nineteenth century wrote many fine poems on rural themes, *was* confined for decades to an insane asylum.

2.  Appositives often come between a subject and a verb. Appositives are nouns, pronouns, or noun phrases that are placed next to nouns to describe them further.

    **Wrong:**        John Smith, *the man who led British expeditions to several American sites*, have left several written accounts of dramatic events there.

    **Correct:**      John Smith, the man who led British expeditions to several American sites, *has* left several written accounts of dramatic events there.

Relative clauses and appositives are sometimes set off from the rest of the sentence by commas. When this is the case, it's a dead giveaway that those words are not part of the subject. That makes checking for subject-verb agreement much easier; just ignore the words set off by commas and concentrate on the subject and the verb.

3.  The prepositional phrase is an all-time favorite.

    **Wrong:**        Wild animals *in jungles all over the world* is endangered.

    **Correct:**      Wild animals in jungles all over the world *are* endangered.

Prepositional phrases, and some relative clauses and appositives, are not set off by commas. It's harder to recognize intervening phrases and clauses when they're not set off by commas, but if you remember to check each sentence carefully for such things, you'll be able to pick them out anyway.

## COMPOUND SUBJECTS

When two nouns or groups of nouns are joined by *and*, they're called a compound subject and are, therefore, plural.

**Correct:** *Ontario and Quebec* contain about two thirds of the population of Canada.

Some connecting phrases may look as though they should make a group of words into a compound subject—but they don't result in a compound subject.

**Wrong:** George Bernard Shaw, as well as Mahatma Gandhi and River Phoenix, were vegetarians.

*And* is the only connecting word that results in a compound and plural subject. The following words and phrases do not create compound subjects:

| | |
|---|---|
| *along with* | *as well as* |
| *together with* | *besides* |
| *in addition to* | |

**Correct:** *George Bernard Shaw*, as well as Mahatma Gandhi and River Phoenix, *was* a vegetarian.

**Wrong:** Neither Thomas Jefferson nor Alexander Hamilton were supportive of Aaron Burr's political ambitions.

When words in the subject position are connected by *either . . . or* or *neither . . . nor*, the verb agrees with the last word in the pair. If the last word is singular, the verb must be singular. If the last word is plural, the verb must be plural.

**Correct:** Neither Thomas Jefferson nor *Alexander Hamilton was* supportive of Aaron Burr's political ambitions.

| Correct: | Neither Thomas Jefferson nor *the Federalists were* supportive of Aaron Burr's political ambitions. |
|---|---|

*Both . . . and* is the only pair that always results in a plural subject.

| Correct: | *Both* Thomas Jefferson *and* Alexander Hamilton *were* unsupportive of Aaron Burr's political ambitions. |
|---|---|

## UNUSUAL SENTENCE PATTERNS

When you're checking for subject-verb disagreement, remember that the subject doesn't always appear before the verb.

| Wrong: | Dominating the New York skyline is the Empire State Building and the Chrysler Building. |
|---|---|

The subject of this sentence is a compound subject, *the Empire State Building and the Chrysler Building*. The verb should be plural.

| Correct: | Dominating the New York skyline *are* the Empire State Building and the Chrysler Building. |
|---|---|

## SUBJECTS THAT ARE NOT NOUNS OR PRONOUNS

An entire clause can serve as the subject of a sentence. When used as subject, a clause always takes a singular verb:

> Whether the economy will improve in the near future *is* a matter of great concern.

Infinitives and gerunds can be used as subjects. Remember that they're singular subjects:

> *To err* is human.
> *Rollerblading* is dangerous.

See the section on verbs for more on infinitives and gerunds.

# MODIFICATION

Adjectives and adverbs aren't the only sentence elements whose job is to modify.
Phrases and even relative clauses can act as modifiers in a sentence. The following
sentence contains several types of modifiers:

> Waiting to regain enough strength to eat, a cheetah, which expends most of
> its energy in the chase, must rest beside its prey.

*Waiting to regain enough strength to eat* is a phrase that describes the cheetah, as does
the relative clause *which expends most of its energy in the chase*. The phrase *beside its prey*
modifies the verb *rest*.

English depends heavily on word order to establish modifying relationships. In other
words, most modifiers attach themselves to the first things they can get their hands on
in the sentence, even if it's the wrong thing.

## INTRODUCTORY MODIFIERS

**Wrong:** Sifting the sand of a river bed, gold was discovered by prospectors
in California in 1848.

A modifying phrase that begins a sentence refers to the noun or pronoun immediately
following the phrase. But if we apply that rule here, the sentence says that the *gold was
sifting sand*. See the problem? The author apparently meant to say that the prospectors
were sifting sand. There are several ways to correct the sentence so that it expresses the
intended meaning.

**Correct:** Sifting the sand in a river bed, prospectors discovered gold in
California in 1848.

**Also Correct:** Prospectors, sifting the sand in a river bed, discovered gold in
California in 1848.

**Also Correct:** Gold was discovered by prospectors, who were sifting the sand in
a river bed, in California in 1848.

In all three cases, the phrase or clause directly precedes or follows the noun it describes.

## DANGLING MODIFIERS

A modifying phrase or clause should clearly refer to a particular word in the sentence. A modifying phrase or clause that does not sensibly refer to any word in the sentence is called a dangling modifier. The most common sort of dangler is an introductory modifying phrase that's followed by a word it can't logically refer to.

**Wrong:** Desiring to free his readers from superstition, the theories of Epicurus are expounded in Lucretius's poem *De rerum natura*.

The problem with this sentence is that the phrase that begins the sentence seems to modify the noun following it: *theories*. In fact, there is really nowhere the modifier can be put to make it work properly and no noun to which it can reasonably refer (*Lucretius's*, the possessive, is functioning as an adjective modifying *poem*). Get rid of dangling constructions by clarifying the modification relationship or by making the dangler into a subordinate clause.

**Correct:** Desiring to free his readers from superstition, Lucretius expounded the theories of Epicurus in his poem *De rerum natura*.

Now the phrase *desiring to free his readers from superstition* clearly refers to the proper noun *Lucretius*.

## OTHER MODIFIERS

In correcting some of those misplaced introductory modifiers, we move the modifier to a position inside the sentence rather than at the beginning. This is perfectly acceptable, but just remember that modifying phrases inside a sentence can also be misplaced.

**Wrong:** That night they sat discussing when the cow might calve in the kitchen.

The problem here is the phrase *in the kitchen*, which seems to refer to where the cow might have her calf. What the author probably meant to say is the following correct sentence:

**Correct:** That night they sat in the kitchen discussing when the cow might calve.

This sentence is correct because the phrase comes directly after the word it modifies: the verb *sat*.

> **Wrong:** As a young man, the French novelist Gustave Flaubert traveled in Egypt, which was a fascinating experience.

It's not that *Egypt* itself was a fascinating experience but that traveling there was fascinating.

> **Correct:** Traveling in Egypt as a young man was a fascinating experience for the French novelist Gustave Flaubert.

# PRONOUNS

When doing Sentence Correction questions, always try to locate the antecedent of a pronoun (that is, the word to which the pronoun refers). Most of the pronoun problems you'll encounter on the test result from a problem in the relationship of the pronoun and its antecedent.

## PRONOUN REFERENCE

In GMAT English, a pronoun must refer clearly to one and only one antecedent.

1. Watch out for sentences in which pronouns refer to indefinite antecedents, paying particular attention to the pronoun *they*. (Avoid references to some vague *they*.)

> **Wrong:** They serve meals on many of the buses that run from Santiago to Antofagasta. (Who are *they*?)

> **Better:** Meals are served on many of the buses that run from Santiago to Antofagasta.

*Note:* It's quite all right to use *it* like this:

> *It* seldom rains in Death Valley.

2. Sometimes a sentence is structured so that a pronoun can refer to more than one thing, and as a result, the reader doesn't know what the author intended.

**Wrong:** Pennsylvania Governor William Keith encouraged the young Benjamin Franklin to open his own printing shop because he perceived that the quality of printing in Philadelphia was poor. (*Which* man perceived that the quality of printing in Philadelphia was poor?)

Pronouns are assumed to refer to the nearest reasonable antecedent. Nonetheless, it is best to avoid structural ambiguity of the sort that occurs in the sentence above.

**Better:** Because *he* perceived that the quality of printing in Philadelphia was poor, Pennsylvania Governor *William Keith* encouraged the young Benjamin Franklin to open his own printing shop. (*Keith* perceived that the quality of printing was poor.)

**Better:** Because the young *Benjamin Franklin* perceived that the quality of printing in Philadelphia was poor, Pennsylvania Governor William Keith encouraged *him* to open *his* own printing shop. (In this version, *Franklin* is the one who perceived that the printing was poor.)

3. Sometimes it's easy to see what the author meant to use for the antecedent, but when you examine the sentence more closely, that antecedent is nowhere to be found. Correct the problem either by replacing the pronoun with a noun or by providing a clear antecedent.

**Poor:** The proslavery writer A. C. C. Thompson questioned Frederick Douglass's authorship of *The Narrative*, claiming that he was too uneducated to have written such an eloquent book.

What's the antecedent of *he*? It should be the noun *Frederick Douglass*, but the sentence contains only the possessive form *Douglass's*. As a rule, avoid using a possessive form as the antecedent of a personal pronoun.

**Better:** The proslavery writer A. C. C. Thompson questioned whether Frederick Douglass actually wrote *The Narrative*, claiming that *he* was too uneducated to have written such an eloquent book.

## ODDBALL PROBLEMS

Here are two oddball pronoun reference problems to watch out for.

### DO SO

| | |
|---|---|
| **Wrong:** | It is common for a native New Yorker who has never driven a car to move to another part of the country and have to learn to do it. |
| **Better:** | It is common for a native New Yorker who has never driven a car to move to another part of the country and have to learn to *do so*. |

### ONE AND YOU

When we give advice to others or make general statements, we often use the pronouns *one* and *you*. "You should brush your teeth every day." "One never knows what to do in a situation like that."

It is never acceptable to mix *one* and *you*, *one* and *yours*, or *you* and *one's* in a sentence together.

| | |
|---|---|
| **Wrong:** | One shouldn't eat a high-fat diet and avoid exercise and then be surprised when you gain weight. |
| **Correct:** | *One* shouldn't eat a high-fat diet and avoid exercise and then be surprised when *one* gains weight. |
| **Also Correct:** | *You* shouldn't eat a high-fat diet and avoid exercise and then be surprised when *you* gain weight. |

Also, never use *one* or *one's* to refer to any antecedent except *one*.

| | |
|---|---|
| **Wrong:** | A person should leave a light on in an empty house if one wants to give the impression that someone is at home. |
| **Correct:** | A *person* should leave a light on in an empty house if *he or she* wants to give the impression that someone is at home. |
| **Also Correct:** | *One* should leave a light on in an empty house if *one* wants to give the impression that someone is at home. |
| **Also Correct:** | *One* should leave a light on in an empty house if *he or she* wants to give the impression that someone is at home. |

## PRONOUN AGREEMENT

Always use singular pronouns to refer to singular entities and plural pronouns to refer to plural entities. First, identify the antecedent of a given pronoun. Don't allow yourself to be distracted by a phrase that comes between the two. The GMAT will frequently try to confuse you by inserting a phrase containing plural nouns between a pronoun and its singular antecedent or vice versa.

| | |
|---|---|
| **Wrong:** | A cactus will flower in spite of the fact that they receive little water. |
| **Correct:** | A *cactus* will flower in spite of the fact that *it* receives little water. |
| **Wrong:** | The number of people with college degrees is many times what they were last summer. |
| **Correct:** | The *number* of people with college degrees is many times what *it* was last summer. |

*Note: The number* is always singular. (The number of cookies he ate *was* impressive.)
*A number* is always plural. (A number of turkeys *were* gathered outside the shed.)

## PRONOUN CASE

One type of pronoun problem you can't catch by looking at the relationship between a pronoun and its antecedent is wrong case.

| | Subjective Case | Objective Case |
|---|---|---|
| First Person: | I, we | me, us |
| Second Person: | you | you |
| Third Person: | he, she, it, they, one | him, her, it, them, one |
| Relative Pronouns: | who, that, which | whom, that, which |

### When to Use Subjective Case Pronouns

1. Use the subjective case for the subject of a sentence:

   *She* is falling asleep.

2. Use the subjective case after forms of *to be*:

   It is *I*.

3. Use the subjective case in comparisons between the subjects of understood verbs:

Gary is taller than *I* (am).

## When to Use Objective Case Pronouns

1. Use the objective case for the object of a verb:

I called *him*.

2. Use the objective case for the object of a preposition:

I laughed at *her*.

3. Use the objective case after infinitives and gerunds:

Asking *him* to go was a big mistake.

4. Use the objective case in comparisons between objects of understood verbs:

She calls you more than (she calls) *me*.

There probably won't be many times when you are in doubt as to which case of a pronoun is correct. However, the following hints may prove helpful.

When two or more nouns or pronouns are functioning the same way in a sentence, determine the correct case of any pronoun by considering it separately:

Beatrice and (*I* or *me*) are going home early.

Without *Beatrice*, should the sentence read: *Me am going home early* or *I am going home early*? *I am going*, of course, so *Beatrice and I are going home early.*

A common mistake in the use of RELATIVE PRONOUNS is using *who* (subject case) when *whom* (object case) is needed or vice versa. If you tend to confuse the two, try the following system.

Scholars have disagreed over (*who* or *whom*) is most likely to have written *A Yorkshire Tragedy*, but some early sources attribute it to Shakespeare.

1. Isolate the relative pronoun in its own clause: *who/whom is most likely to have written* A Yorkshire Tragedy.

2. Ask yourself the question: Who or whom wrote *A Yorkshire Tragedy*?

3. Answer with an ordinary personal pronoun: *He* did. (If you are a native speaker of English, your ear undoubtedly tells you that *him did* is wrong.)

4. Since *he* is in the subjective case, we need the subjective case relative pronoun: *who*. Therefore this sentence should read as follows:

> Scholars have disagreed over *who* is most likely to have written *A Yorkshire Tragedy*, but some early sources attribute it to Shakespeare.

# VERBS

Here are some important terms and concepts to review before you read this section:

> **Verb:** A word that expresses an action or a state of being

> **Verbal:** A word that is formed from a verb but is not functioning as a verb. There are three kinds of verbals: *participles, gerunds,* and *infinitives.*

It is important to realize that a verbal is not a verb, because a sentence must contain a verb and a verbal won't do. A group of words containing a verbal but lacking a verb is not a sentence.

**Participle:** Usually ends in *-ing* or *-ed*. It is used as an adjective in a sentence:

> Let *sleeping* dogs lie.
>
> It is difficult to calm a *frightened* child.
>
> *Peering* into his microscope, Robert Koch saw the tuberculosis bacilli.

**Gerund:** Always ends in *-ing*. It is used in a sentence as a noun:

> *Skiing* can be dangerous.
>
> *Raising* a family is a serious task.
>
> I was surprised at his *acting* like such a coward.

Note from the third sentence that a noun or pronoun that comes before a gerund is in the possessive form: *his*, not *him*.

**Infinitive:** The basic form of a verb, generally preceded by *to*. It is usually used as a noun but may be used as an adjective or an adverb.

> Winston Churchill liked *to paint*. (Infinitive used as a noun.)
>
> The will *to conquer* is crucial. (Infinitive used as an adjective—modifies the *will*.)

Students in imperial China studied the Confucian classics *to excel* on civil service exams. (Infinitive used as an adverb—modifies *studied*.)

## VERB TENSE

On the GMAT, you'll find items that are wrong because a verb is in the wrong tense. To spot this kind of problem, you need to be familiar with both the way each tense is used individually and the ways the tenses are used together.

### Present Tense

Use the present tense to describe a state or action occurring in the present time:

Congress *is* debating health policy this session.

Use the present tense to describe habitual action:

Many Americans *jog* every day.

Use the present tense to describe "general truths"—things that are always true:

The earth *is* round and *rotates* on its axis.

### Past Tense

Use the simple past tense to describe an event or state that took place at a specific time in the past and is now over and done with:

Hundreds of people *died* when the Titanic sank.
Few people *bought* new cars last year.

There are two other ways to express past action:

Bread *used to* cost a few cents per loaf.
George Bush *did promise* not to raise taxes.

### Future Tense

Use the future tense for intended actions or actions expected in the future:

The twenty-second century *will begin* in the year 2101.

We often express future actions with the expression *to be going to*:

I *am going to move* to another apartment as soon as possible.

The simple present tense is also used to speak of future events. This is called the anticipatory future. We often use the anticipatory future with verbs of motion, such as *come, go, arrive, depart*, and *leave*:

The senator *is leaving* for Europe tomorrow.

We also use the anticipatory future in two-clause sentences when one verb is in the regular future tense:

The disputants will announce the new truce as soon as they *agree* on its terms.

## Present Perfect Tense

Use the present perfect tense for actions and states that started in the past and continue up to and into the present time:

Hawaii *has been* a state since 1959.

Use the present perfect for actions and states that happen a number of times in the past and may happen again in the future:

Italy *has had* many changes in government since World War II.

Use the present perfect for something that happened at an unspecified time in the past. Notice the difference in meaning between the two sample sentences below:

**Present Perfect:** Susan Sontag *has written* a critical essay about Leni Riefenstahl. (We have no idea when—we just know she wrote it.)

**Simple Past:** Susan Sontag *wrote* a critical essay about Leni Riefenstahl in 1974. (We use the simple past because we're specifying when Sontag wrote the essay.)

## Past Perfect Tense

The past perfect tense is used to represent past actions or states that were completed before other past actions or states. The more recent past event is expressed in the simple past, and the earlier past event is expressed in the past perfect:

After he came to America, Vladimir Nabokov translated novels that *he had written* in Russian while he was living in Europe.

Note the difference in meaning between these two sentences:

The Civil War *had ended* when Lincoln was shot. = *The war was over by the time of Lincoln's death.*

The Civil War *ended* when Lincoln was shot. = *The war ended when Lincoln died.*

### Future Perfect Tense

Use the future perfect tense for a future state or event that will take place before another future event:

By the time the next election is held, the candidates *will have debated* at least once. (Note that the present tense form [anticipatory future] is used in the first clause.)

## SEQUENCE OF TENSES

When a sentence has two or more verbs in it, you should always check to see whether the tenses of those verbs correctly indicate the order in which things happened. As a general rule, if two things happened at the same time, the verbs should be in the same tense.

**Wrong:** Just as the sun rose, the rooster crows.

*Rose* is past tense and *crows* is present tense, but the words *just as* indicate that both things happened at the same time. The verbs should be in the same tense.

**Correct:** Just as the sun *rose*, the rooster *crowed*.

**Also Correct:** Just as the sun *rises*, the rooster *crows*.

When we're talking about the past or the future, we often want to indicate that one thing happened or will happen before another. That's where the past perfect and the future perfect come in.

Use the past perfect for the earlier of two past events and the simple past for the later event.

>   **Wrong:**     Mozart finished about two thirds of the Requiem when he died.

Putting both verbs of the sentence in the simple past tense makes it sound as if Mozart wrote two thirds of the Requiem after dying. If we put the first verb into the past perfect, though, the sentence makes much more sense.

>   **Correct:**   Mozart *had finished* about two thirds of the Requiem when he *died*.

*Note:* Occasionally, the GMAT won't use the past perfect for the earlier event. It will use a word like *before* or *after* to make the sequence of events clear. You should always look for the past perfect, but if it's not there, you can settle for the simple past with a time word such as *before* or *after*.

Use the future perfect for the earlier of two future events.

>   **Wrong:**     By the time I write to Leo, he will probably move.

The point the author is trying to get across is not that Leo will move when he gets the letter but that by the time the letter arrives, he'll be living somewhere else.

>   **Correct:**   By the time I write to Leo, he *will* probably *have moved*.

When you use a participial phrase in a sentence, the action or the situation that phrase describes is assumed to take place at the same time as the action or state described by the verb of the sentence.

>   **Wrong:**     Being a French colony, Senegal is a Francophone nation.

This implies that Senegal is still a French colony. We can make the information in the participial phrase refer to an earlier time than does the verb by changing the regular participle to what's called a perfect participle. The way to do it is to use *having* + *the past participle*.

>   **Correct:**   *Having been a French colony*, Senegal is a Francophone nation.

You can do the same thing with infinitives by replacing the regular infinitive with *to have + the past participle:*

> I'm glad *to meet you.* (I'm glad to be in the process of meeting you right now.)
>
> I'm glad *to have* met you. (I'm glad now that I met you earlier today, last week, or whenever.)

## SUBJUNCTIVE MOOD

On the GMAT, you may come across an item that tests your knowledge of the subjunctive. Subjunctive verb forms are used in two ways.

The subjunctive form *were* is used in statements that express a wish or situations that are contrary to fact:

> I wish I *were* a rich man. (But I'm not.)
>
> If I *were* you, I wouldn't do that. (But I'm not you.)

The subjunctive of requirement is used after verbs such as *ask, demand, insist,* and *suggest*—or after expressions of requirement, suggestion, or demand. A subjunctive verb of requirement is in the base form of the verb; that is, the infinitive without *to:*

> Airlines insist that each passenger *pass* through a metal detector.
>
> It's extremely important that silicon chips *be made* in a dust-free environment.

## CONDITIONAL SENTENCES

Conditional sentences are if-then statements:

> *If* you go, *then* I'll go, too.

We use conditional sentences when we want to speculate about the results of a particular situation. There are three types of conditional sentences.

**Statements of Fact:** There is a real possibility that the situation described in the *if* clause really happened, is happening, or will happen:

> If Vladimir Putin resigns, there will be unrest in Russia.
>
> If John Milton met Galileo, they probably discussed astronomy.

**Contrary to Fact:** The situation in the *if* clause never happened, so what is said in the *then* clause is pure speculation:

> Blaise Pascal wrote that if Cleopatra's nose had been shorter, the face of the world would have changed.

> Alexander the Great said, "If I were not Alexander, I would want to be Diogenes."

**Future Speculation:** Some conditional sentences speculate about the future but with the idea that the situation in the *if* clause is extremely unlikely to happen:

> If Shakespeare's manuscripts were to be discovered, the texts of some of his plays would be less uncertain.

# PARALLELISM

Remember, when you express a number of ideas of equal importance and function in the same sentence, you should always be careful to make them all the same grammatical form (that is, all nouns, all adjectives, all gerunds, all clauses, or whatever). That's called parallel structure or parallelism.

## COORDINATE IDEAS

Coordinate ideas occur in pairs or in series, and they are linked by conjunctions such as *and*, *but*, *or*, and *nor*, or, in certain instances, by linking verbs such as *is*.

| **Wrong:** | To earn credits, an American college student can take up folk dancing, ballet, or study belly dancing. |
|---|---|
| **Correct:** | To earn credits, an American college student can take up *folk dancing*, *ballet*, or *belly dancing*. |

Note that once you begin repeating a word in a series like the following, you must follow through:

| **Wrong:** | A wage earner might invest her money in stocks, in bonds, or real estate. |
|---|---|
| **Correct:** | A wage earner might invest her money *in* stocks, *in* bonds, or *in* real estate. |

**Also Correct:**   A wage earner might invest her money *in* stocks, bonds, or real estate.

This principle applies equally to prepositions (*in, on, by, with*, etc.), articles (*the, a, an*), helping verbs (*had, has, would*, etc.), and possessive pronouns (*his, her*, etc.). You must either repeat the preposition, helping verb, or whatever in front of each element in the series or include it only in front of the first item in the series.

## CORRELATIVE CONSTRUCTIONS

There is a group of words in English that are called correlative conjunctions. They are used to relate two ideas in some way. Here's a list of them:

> *both . . . and*
> *either . . . or*
> *neither . . . nor*
> *not only . . . but (also)*

You should always be careful to place correlative conjunctions immediately before the terms they're coordinating.

**Wrong:**        Isaac Newton not only studied physics but also theology.

The problem here is that the author intends to coordinate the two nouns *physics* and *theology* but makes the mistake of putting the verb of the sentence (*studied*) after the first element of the construction (*not only*) and in so doing destroys the parallelism. Note that the solution to an error like this is usually to move one of the conjunctions.

**Correct:**        Isaac Newton studied not only *physics* but also *theology*.

## COMPARED OR CONTRASTED IDEAS

Frequently, two or more ideas are compared or contrasted within the same sentence. Compared or contrasted ideas should be presented in the same grammatical form.

Certain phrases should clue you in that the sentence contains ideas that should be presented in parallel form. These phrases include *as . . . as* and *more (or less)* x *than* y.

| **Wrong:** | Skiing is as strenuous as to run. |
| **Correct:** | *Skiing* is as strenuous as *running*. |
| **Wrong:** | Skiing is less dangerous than to rappel down a cliff. |
| **Correct:** | *To ski* is less dangerous than *to rappel* down a cliff. |

### To Be

In certain cases, sentences with forms of *to be* must be expressed in parallel form.

| **Wrong:** | To drive while intoxicated is risking grave injury and criminal charges. |

When an infinitive is the subject of *to be*, don't use a gerund after the verb and vice versa. Pair infinitives with infinitives and gerunds with gerunds.

| **Correct:** | *To drive* while intoxicated is *to risk* grave injury and criminal charges. |

Note that we wouldn't change both words to gerunds in this sentence because it wouldn't sound idiomatic.

# COMPARISONS

On the GMAT, you will see a number of sentences that make comparisons. A sentence that makes a comparison must do two things: it must be clear about what is being compared, and it must compare things that logically can be compared. A sentence that makes an unclear or illogical comparison is grammatically unacceptable. When you see a comparative expression such as *like, as, more than, unlike, less than, similar to,* or *different from*, it should remind you to ask yourself two questions about the comparison in the sentence: Is it clear? Is it logical?

## UNCLEAR COMPARISONS

Sometimes it isn't clear what the author is trying to compare.

| **Wrong:** | Byron admired Dryden more than Wordsworth. |

There are two ways to interpret this sentence: that Dryden meant more to Byron than Wordsworth did, or that Byron thought more highly of Dryden than Wordsworth did. Whichever meaning you choose, the problem can be cleared up by adding more words to the sentence.

**Correct:** Byron admired Dryden more than *he did* Wordsworth.

**Also Correct:** Byron admired Dryden more than *Wordsworth did*.

## ILLOGICAL COMPARISONS

Sometimes what the author meant to say is clear enough, but what the author meant to say is not what he or she ended up saying.

**Wrong:** The peaches here are riper than any other fruitstand.

This sentence is comparing *peaches* to *fruitstands*, even though that's clearly not the intention of the author. We can correct it so that we're comparing peaches to peaches by inserting the phrase *those at*.

**Correct:** The peaches here are riper than *those at* any other fruitstand.

Now the pronoun *those* is standing in for *peaches*, so the sentence is accurately comparing things that can be reasonably compared: the peaches here and some other peaches.

Incomplete comparisons like this one are normally corrected by inserting a phrase like *those of, those in, those at, that of, that in*, and *that at*.

Incomplete comparisons can also be corrected by use of the possessive.

**Wrong:** Many critics considered Enrico Caruso's voice better than any other tenor. (This is comparing a voice to a person.)

**Correct:** Many critics considered Enrico Caruso's voice better than *any other tenor's*. (Note that this is a shortened version of *Many critics considered Enrico Caruso's voice better than any other tenor's voice.*)

The second sort of incomplete comparison occurs when one thing is being compared to a group it is a part of. This error is corrected by inserting either the word *other* or the word *else*.

**Wrong:** Astaire danced better than any man in the world.

This is wrong because he couldn't have danced better than himself.

**Correct:** Astaire danced better than any *other* man in the world.

## COMPARATIVE FORMS

The comparative form is used when comparing only two members of a class, and the superlative is used for three or more.

Loretta's grass grows *more vigorously* than Jim's.

Loretta's grass grows the *most vigorously* of any in the neighborhood.

Of Buchanan and Lincoln, the *latter* was *taller*.

Of McKinley, Roosevelt, and Taft, the *last* was *heaviest*.

## IDIOM

Sometimes the right way to say something isn't a matter of grammar but is a matter of idiom: an accepted, set phrase or usage that's right for no other reason than that's just the way we say it.

Most of what we call "idioms" are pairs of words that are used together to convey a particular meaning, and many "idiom errors" result from substituting an unacceptable word—usually a preposition—for a word that is always part of the idiom.

**Wrong:** Brigitte Bardot has joined an organization that is concerned in preventing cruelty to animals.

The adjective *concerned* is followed by either *about* or *with*, either of which would be idiomatic here. But the expression *concerned in* simply isn't idiomatic—we just don't say it that way.

**Correct:** Brigitte Bardot has joined an organization that is *concerned with* preventing cruelty to animals.

**Also Correct:** Brigitte Bardot has joined an organization that is *concerned about* preventing cruelty to animals.

There are so many possible idiom errors of this kind that we can't list them all. The most frequently tested errors, however, are contained in Appendix 3: Common GMAT Idioms.

# ELLIPSIS

An ellipsis is the omission from a sentence of words that are clearly understood. Ellipsis is perfectly acceptable as long as it's done properly—in fact, we do it all the time. Not many people would make a statement like this:

> I've seen more movies this year than you have seen movies this year.

Instead, we would automatically shorten the statement to this much more concise and natural sounding one:

> I've seen more movies this year than you have.

In the following sentence, ellipsis is properly used:

> *The Spectator* was written by Addison and Steele.

This is a shorter way of saying:

> *The Spectator* was written by Addison and by Steele.

It's all right to leave the second *by* out of the sentence because the same preposition appears before *Addison* and before *Steele*, so you need to use it only once.

Now watch what happens when ellipsis is improperly used.

> **Wrong:**     Ezra Pound was interested but not very knowledgeable about economics.

This is wrong because the preposition that's needed after the word *interested* (*in*) is not the same as the preposition that follows the word *knowledgeable* (*about*).

> **Correct:**     Ezra Pound was *interested in* but not very *knowledgeable about* economics.

> **Wrong:**     London always has and always will be the capital of the United Kingdom.

This is wrong because the verb form that's needed after *has* is not the same as the one that's needed after *will*, so both must be included.

> **Correct:**     London *always has been* and *always will be* the capital of the United Kingdom.

## NEGATIVES

You will probably run across at least one item that tests your ability to recognize the difference between idiomatic and unidiomatic ways to express negative ideas. You already know that a double negative is a no-no in standard written English. You wouldn't have any trouble realizing that a sentence such as "I don't want no help," is unacceptable. But the incorrect negatives you will probably see on the exam won't be quite that obvious.

The obviously negative words are *neither, nobody, nor, nowhere, never, none, not, no one,* and *nothing*. But don't forget that *barely, rarely, without, hardly, seldom,* and *scarcely* are also grammatically negative.

In Sentence Correction, you'll find problems with these words where sentences connect two or three negative ideas. Read through the following example sentences carefully:

> There were *neither* threats *nor* bombing campaigns.
> There were *no* threats *or* bombing campaigns.
> There were *no* threats *and no* bombing campaigns.
> There were *no* threats, *nor* were there bombing campaigns.

These are the most common idiomatic ways to join two negative ideas. If you can remember these patterns, you can probably eliminate many wrong answers, because they in some way violate these idiomatic patterns.

**Wrong:** When Walt Whitman's family moved to Brooklyn, there were no bridges nor tunnels across the East River.

The phrase *no bridges nor tunnels* is just not idiomatic—it contains a double negative. The sentence can be rewritten to correct the problem in several ways.

**Correct:** There were *no bridges or tunnels* across the East River.

**Also Correct:** There were *neither bridges nor tunnels* across the East River.

**Also Correct:** There were *no bridges and no tunnels* across the East River.

Another situation in which negatives can cause problems is in a series. Words like *no, not,* and *without* must follow the same rules as prepositions, articles, helping verbs, and the like.

**Wrong:**    After the floods in the Midwest, many farmers were left without homes, businesses, and huge bills to replace all they had lost.

When a preposition, such as *without* in this sentence, is used in front of only the first member of a series, it's taken to refer to all three members of the series. Here, that causes the sentence to say that the farmers were left without homes, without businesses, and without huge bills to replace what they had lost, which makes no sense. There are several ways to rewrite the sentence so that it makes sense.

**Correct:**    After the floods in the Midwest, many farmers were left *without* homes, *without* businesses, and *with* huge bills to replace all they had lost.

**Also Correct:**  After the floods in the Midwest, many farmers were left *with no* homes, *with no* businesses, and *with* huge bills to replace all they had lost.

**Also Correct:**  After the floods in the Midwest, many farmers were left *with no* homes, *no* businesses, and huge bills to replace all they had lost.

# APPENDIX 2: GUIDE TO USAGE AND STYLE

In chapter 2, we discussed how to analyze a GMAT essay topic, organize your thoughts, and outline an essay. Once you have an overall idea of what you want to say in your essay, you can start thinking about how to say it. This appendix emphasizes the skills you need for the second stage of the writing process: producing clearly developed and well-organized essays. The best strategy is to study this section and tackle the exercises in short, manageable blocks, interspersed with the study of other subjects in preparation for the GMAT.

Perhaps the single most important thing to bear in mind when writing essays is this: *Keep it simple.* This applies to word choice, sentence structure, and argument. Obsession about how to spell a word correctly can throw off your flow of thought. The more complicated (and wordy) your sentences, the more likely they will contain errors. The more convoluted your argument, the more likely you will get bogged down in convoluted sentence structure. Yet recall that simple does *not* mean simplistic. A clear, straightforward approach can be sophisticated.

Many students mistakenly believe that their essays will be "downgraded" by such mechanical errors as misplaced commas, poor choice of words, misspellings, faulty grammar, and so on. Occasional problems of this type will not significantly affect your GMAT essay score. The test readers understand that you are writing first-draft essays. They will *not* be looking to take points off for such errors, unless the writer makes them repeatedly. If an essay is littered with misspellings, incorrect usage, and the like, then a more serious communication problem is indicated.

Bottom line: Don't worry excessively about writing mechanics but do try to train yourself out of poor habits and do proofread your essays for obvious errors. Your objective in taking the GMAT is admission to business school. To achieve that objective, give the business schools what they want. They do not expect eloquence in a 30-minute assignment, but they do want to see effective writing.

To write an effective essay, there are three things you need to do:

1. Be concise.
2. Be forceful.
3. Be correct.

An effective essay is concise; it wastes no words. An effective essay is forceful; it makes its point. And an effective essay is correct; it conforms to the generally accepted rules of grammar and form.

The following pages break down the three broad objectives of concision, forcefulness, and correctness into 16 specific principles. Don't panic! Many of them will already be familiar to you. And, besides, you will have many chances to practice in the exercises we provide.

Principles 1 through 4 aim primarily at the first objective, concise writing; principles 5 through 10 aim primarily at the second objective, forceful writing; and principles 11 through 16 aim primarily at the third objective, grammatically correct writing. For a thorough understanding of the third of these objectives, though, you should consult appendix 1, the Grammar Reference Guide. In this appendix, we concentrate on principles that are rarely tested in Sentence Correction but become important when you do your writing. Each principle is illustrated by exercises. (Answers to these exercises are at the end of this section.)

The principles of concise and forceful writing are generally not as rigid as the principles of grammatically correct writing. Concision and forcefulness are matters of art and personal style, as well as common sense and tradition. But if you are going to disregard a principle, we hope you will do so out of educated choice. On the GMAT Analytical Writing Assessment, sticking closely to the principles of standard English writing should produce a concise, forceful, and correct essay.

## BE CONCISE

The first four principles of good writing relate to the goal of expressing your points clearly in as few words as possible. Each principle represents a specific way to tighten up your writing.

# PRINCIPLE 1: AVOID WORDINESS

Do not use several words when one will do. Wordy phrases are like junk food: they add only fat, not muscle. Many people make the mistake of writing phrases such as *at the present time* or *at this point in time* instead of the simpler *now*, or *take into consideration* instead of simply *consider*, in an attempt to make their prose seem more scholarly or more formal. It does not work. Instead, their prose ends up seeming inflated and pretentious. Don't waste your words or your time.

| | |
|---|---|
| **Wordy:** | I am of the opinion that the aforementioned managers should be advised that they will be evaluated with regard to the utilization of responsive organizational software for the purpose of devising a responsive network of customers. |
| **Concise:** | We should tell the managers that we will evaluate their use of flexible computerized databases to develop a customer network. |

## Exercise 1: Wordy Phrases

Improve the following sentences by omitting or replacing wordy phrases:

1. In view of the fact that John has prepared with much care for this presentation, it would be a good idea to award him with the project.


2. The airline has a problem with always having arrivals that come at least an hour late, despite the fact that the leaders of the airline promise that promptness is a goal which has a high priority for all the employees involved.


3. In spite of the fact that she only has a little bit of experience in photography right now, she will probably do well in the future because she has a great deal of motivation to succeed in her chosen profession.


4. Accuracy is a subject that has great importance to English teachers and company presidents alike.

5. The reason why humans kill each other is that they experience fear of those whom they do not understand.

---

## PRINCIPLE 2: DON'T BE REDUNDANT

Redundancy means that the writer needlessly repeats an idea. It's redundant to speak of "a beginner lacking experience." The word *beginner* implies lack of experience by itself. You can eliminate redundant words or phrases without changing the meaning of the sentence. Watch out for words that add nothing to the sense of the sentence.

Here are some common redundancies:

| Redundant | Concise |
|---|---|
| *refer back* | *refer* |
| *few in number* | *few* |
| *small-sized* | *small* |
| *grouped together* | *grouped* |
| *end result* | *result* |

Redundancy often results from carelessness, but you can easily eliminate redundant elements when proofreading.

### Exercise 2: Redundancy

Repair the following sentences by crossing out redundant elements:

1. All these problems have combined together to create a serious crisis.

2. A staff that large in size needs an effective supervisor who can get the job done.

3. He knows how to follow directions, and he knows how to do what he is told.

4. The recently observed trend of spending on credit has created a middle class that is poorer and more impoverished than ever before.

5. Those who can follow directions are few in number.

## PRINCIPLE 3: AVOID NEEDLESS QUALIFICATION

Since the object of your essay is to convince your reader, you will want to adopt a reasonable tone. There will likely be no single, clear-cut "answer" to the essay topic, so don't overstate your case. Occasional use of such qualifiers as *fairly*, *rather*, *somewhat*, and *relatively* and of such expressions as *seems to be*, *a little*, and *a certain amount of* will let the reader know you are reasonable, but overusing such modifiers weakens your argument. Excessive qualification makes you sound hesitant. Like wordy phrases, qualifiers can add bulk without adding substance.

**Wordy:** This rather serious breach of etiquette may possibly shake the very foundations of the corporate world.

**Concise:** This serious breach of etiquette may shake the foundations of the corporate world.

Just as bad is the overuse of the word *very*. Some writers use this intensifying adverb before almost every adjective in an attempt to be more forceful. If you need to add emphasis, look for a stronger adjective (or verb).

**Weak:** Novak is a very good pianist.

**Strong:** Novak is a virtuoso pianist.
or
Novak plays beautifully.

And don't try to qualify words that are already absolute.

| Wrong | Correct |
|---|---|
| *more unique* | *unique* |
| *the very worst* | *the worst* |
| *completely full* | *full* |

### Exercise 3: Excessive Qualification

Practice achieving concision by eliminating needless qualification in the sentences below:

1. She is a fairly excellent teacher.

2. Ferrara seems to be sort of a slow worker.

3. You yourself are the very best person to decide what you should do for a living.

4. Needless to say, children should be taught to cooperate at home and in school.

5. The travel agent does not recommend the trip to Tripoli, since it is possible that one may be hurt.

## PRINCIPLE 4: DO NOT WRITE SENTENCES JUST TO FILL UP SPACE

This principle suggests several things:

- Don't write a sentence that gets you nowhere.

- Don't ask a question only to answer it.

- Don't merely copy the essay's directions.

- Don't write a whole sentence only to announce that you're changing the subject.

If you have something to say, say it without preamble. If you need to smooth over a change of subject, do so with a transitional word or phrase rather than with a meaningless sentence. If your proofreading reveals unintentional wasted sentences, neatly cross them out.

**Wordy:**    Which idea of the author's is more in line with what I believe? This is a very interesting . . . .

**Concise:**    The author's beliefs are similar to mine.

The author of the wordy example above is just wasting words and time. Get to the point quickly and stay there. Simplicity and clarity win points.

### Exercise 4: Unnecessary Sentences

Rewrite each of these multiple-sentence statements as one concise sentence:

1. What's the purpose of getting rid of the chemical pollutants in water? People cannot safely consume water that contains chemical pollutants.

2. I do not believe those who argue that some of Shakespeare's plays were written by others. There is no evidence that other people had a hand in writing Shakespeare's plays.

---

3. Which point of view is closest to my own? This is a good question. I agree with those who say that the United States should send soldiers to areas of conflict.

---

4. Frank Lloyd Wright was a famous architect. He was renowned for his ability to design buildings that blend into their surroundings.

---

5. A lot of people find math a difficult subject to master. They have trouble with math because it requires very precise thinking skills.

---

# BE FORCEFUL

The next group of principles aims at the goal of producing forceful writing. If you follow these principles, your writing will be much more convincing to the reader.

## PRINCIPLE 5: AVOID NEEDLESS SELF-REFERENCE

Avoid such unnecessary phrases as "I believe," "I feel," and "in my opinion." There is no need to remind your reader that what you are writing is your opinion.

> **Weak:** I am of the opinion that air pollution is a more serious problem than the government has led us to believe.

> **Forceful:** Air pollution is a more serious problem than the government has led us to believe.

Self-reference is another form of qualifying what you say—a very obvious form. One or two self-references in an essay might be appropriate, just as the use of qualifiers like *probably* and *perhaps* can be effective if you practice using them *sparingly*. Practice is the only sure way to improve your writing.

### Exercise 5: Needless Self-Reference

Eliminate needless self-references in these sentences:

1. I do not think this argument can be generalized to most business owners.

   _____

2. My own experience shows me that food is the best social lubricant.

   _____

3. Although I am no expert, I do not think privacy should be valued more than social concerns.

   _____

4. My guess is that most people want to do good work but many are bored or frustrated with their jobs.

   _____

5. I must emphasize that I am not saying the author does not have a point.

   _____

## PRINCIPLE 6: USE THE ACTIVE VOICE

Using the passive voice is a way to avoid accountability. Put verbs in the active voice whenever possible. In the active voice, the subject performs the action (e.g., we write essays). In the passive voice, the subject is the receiver of the action, and the performer of the action is often only implied (e.g., essays are written).

You should avoid the passive voice *EXCEPT* in the following cases:

- When you do not know who performed the action: *The letter was opened before I received it.* (For example, see the last sentence of the above paragraph.)

- When you prefer not to refer directly to the person who performs the action: *An error has been made in computing this data.*

| | |
|---|---|
| **Passive:** | The estimate of this year's tax revenues was prepared by the General Accounting Office. |
| **Active:** | The General Accounting Office prepared the estimate of this year's tax revenues. |

### Exercise 6: Undesirable Passives

Replace passive voice with active wherever possible:

1. The politician's standing in the polls has been hurt by recent allegations of corruption.

   _____

2. The bill was passed in time, but it was not signed by the president until the time for action had passed.

   _____

3. Advice is usually requested by those who need it least; it is not sought out by the truly lost and ignorant.

   _____

4. The minutes of the city council meeting should be taken by the city clerk.

   _____

5. The report was compiled by a number of field anthropologists and marriage experts.

   _____

## PRINCIPLE 7: AVOID WEAK OPENINGS

Try not to begin a sentence with *there is, there are*, or *it is*. These roundabout expressions usually indicate that you are trying to distance yourself from the position you are taking.

### Exercise 7: Weak Openings

Rewrite these sentences to eliminate weak openings:

1. It would be unwise for businesses to ignore the illiteracy problem.

   _____

2. It would be of no use to fight a drug war without waging a battle against demand for illicit substances.

   _____

3. There are many strong points in the candidate's favor; intelligence, unfortunately, is not among them.

   _____

4. It has been decided that we, as a society, can tolerate homelessness.

   _____

5. There seems to be little doubt that Americans like watching television better than conversing.

   _____

## PRINCIPLE 8: AVOID NEEDLESSLY VAGUE LANGUAGE

Don't just ramble on when you're writing your GMAT essays. Choose specific, descriptive words. Vague language weakens your writing because it forces the reader to guess what you mean instead of concentrating fully on your ideas and style. The essay topics you're given aren't going to be obscure. You will be able to come up with specific examples and concrete information about the topics. Your argument will be more forceful if you stick to this information.

| | |
|---|---|
| **Weak:** | Brown is highly educated. |
| **Forceful:** | Brown has a master's degree in business administration. |
| **Weak:** | She is a great communicator. |
| **Forceful:** | She speaks persuasively. |

Notice that sometimes, to be more specific and concrete, you will have to use more words than you might with vague language. This principle is not in conflict with the general objective of concision. Being concise may mean eliminating unnecessary words. Avoiding vagueness may mean adding necessary words.

### Exercise 8: Needlessly Vague Language

Rewrite these sentences to replace vague language with specific, concrete language:

1. Water is transformed into steam when the former is heated up to 100°C.

_____

2. The diplomat was required to execute an agreement that stipulated that he would live in whatever country the federal government thought necessary.

_____

3. The principal told John that he should not even think about coming back to school until he changed his ways.

_____

4. The police detective had to seek the permission of the lawyer to question the suspect.

_____

5. Thousands of species of animals were destroyed when the last ice age occurred.

_____

## PRINCIPLE 9: AVOID CLICHÉS

Clichés are overused expressions; that is, expressions that may once have seemed colorful and powerful but are now dull and worn out. Time pressure and anxiety may make you lose focus; that's when clichés may slip into your writing. A reliance on clichés will suggest you are a lazy thinker. Keep them out of your essay.

**Weak:**     Performance in a crisis is the acid test for a leader.

**Forceful:**     Performance in a crisis is the best indicator of a leader's abilities.

Putting a cliché in quotation marks to indicate your distance from the cliché does not strengthen the sentence. If anything, it just makes weak writing more noticeable. Notice whether you use clichés. If you do, ask yourself if you could substitute more specific language for the cliché.

### Exercise 9: Clichés

Make the following sentences more forceful by replacing clichés:

1. Beyond the shadow of a doubt, Jefferson was a great leader.

   _____

2. Trying to find the employee responsible for this embarrassing information leak is like trying to find a needle in a haystack.

   _____

3. The military is putting all its eggs in one basket by relying so heavily on nuclear missiles for the nation's defense.

   _____

4. Older doctors should be required to update their techniques, but you can't teach an old dog new tricks.

   _____

5. A ballpark estimate of the number of fans in the stadium would be 120,000.

   _____

## PRINCIPLE 10: AVOID JARGON

Jargon includes two categories of words that you should avoid. First is the specialized vocabulary of a group, such as that used by doctors, lawyers, or baseball coaches. Second is the overly inflated and complex language that burdens many students' essays. You will not impress anyone with big words that do not fit the tone or context of your essay, especially if you misuse them.

If you are not certain of a word's meaning or appropriateness, leave it out. An appropriate word, even a simple one, will add impact to your argument. As you come across words you are unsure of, ask yourself, "Would a reader in a different field be able to understand exactly what I mean from the words I've chosen?" "Is there any way I can say the same thing more simply?"

| | |
|---|---|
| **Weak:** | The international banks are cognizant of the new law's significance. |
| **Forceful:** | The international banks are aware of the new law's significance. |
| **Wrong:** | The new law would negatively impact each of the nations involved. |
| **Correct:** | The new law would hurt each of the nations involved. (*Impact* is also used to mean *affect* or *benefit*.) |

The following are commonly used jargon words:

*prioritize*       *parameter*
*optimize*        *time frame*
*utilize*          *input/output*
*finalize*         *maximize*
*designate*       *facilitate*
*bottom line*

## Exercise 10: Jargon

Replace the jargon in the following sentences with more appropriate language:

1.  We anticipate utilizing hundreds of paper clips in the foreseeable future.

   _____

2.  Education-wise, our schoolchildren have been neglected.

   _____

3.  Foreign diplomats should always interface with local leaders.

   _____

4. There is considerable evidentiary support for the assertion that Vienna sausages are good for you.

---

5. In the case of the recent railway disaster, it is clear that governmental regulatory agencies obfuscated in the preparation of materials for release to the public through both the electronic and print media.

---

# BE CORRECT

Correctness is perhaps the most difficult objective for writers to achieve. The complex rules of standard English usage can leave you feeling unsure of your writing and more than a bit confused. But remember, the most important lesson you can take from this section is how to organize your thoughts into a strong, well-supported argument. Style and grammar are important but secondary concerns. Your readers will *not* mark you down for occasional errors common to first-draft writing. So just think of this section, together with the Grammar Reference Guide, as helping you to improve the details of good writing. If this material begins to overwhelm you, stop and take a break. You need time to absorb this information.

Do the exercises and then compare your answers to ours. Make sure you understand what the error was in each sentence. Use what you learn in this section to help you proofread your practice essays; later, return to your practice essays and edit them. Better yet, ask a friend to edit them, paying special attention to correctness.

## PRINCIPLE 11: AVOID SLANG AND COLLOQUIALISMS

Conversational speech is filled with slang and colloquial expressions. However, you should avoid slang on the GMAT Analytical Writing Assessment. Slang terms and colloquialisms can be confusing to the reader, since these expressions are not universally understood. Even worse, such informal writing may give readers the impression that you are poorly educated or arrogant.

| | |
|---|---|
| **Inappropriate:** | He is really into gardening. |
| **Correct:** | He enjoys gardening. |
| **Inappropriate:** | She plays a wicked game of tennis. |
| **Correct:** | She excels in tennis. |
| **Inappropriate:** | Myra has got to go to Memphis for a week. |
| **Correct:** | Myra must go to Memphis for a week. |
| **Inappropriate:** | Joan has been doing science for eight years now. |
| **Correct:** | Joan has been a scientist for eight years now. |

With a little thought, you will find the right word. Using informal language is risky. Play it safe by sticking to standard usage.

## Exercise 11: Slang and Colloquialisms

Replace the informal elements of the following sentences with more appropriate terms:

1. Cynthia Larson sure knows her stuff.

   _____

2. Normal human beings can't cope with repeated humiliation.

   _____

3. If you want a good cheesecake, you must make a top-notch crust.

   _____

4. International organizations should try and cooperate on global issues like hunger.

   _____

5. The environmentalists aren't in it for the prestige; they really care about protecting the yellow-throated hornswoggler.

   _____

## PRINCIPLE 12: USE COMMAS CORRECTLY

When using the comma, follow these rules:

A. Use commas to separate items in a series. If more than two items are listed in a series, they should be separated by commas; the final comma—the one that precedes the word *and*—is optional. *Never* use a comma after the word *and*.

> **Correct:** My recipe for buttermilk biscuits contains flour, baking soda, salt, shortening, and buttermilk.

> **Correct:** My recipe for chocolate cake contains flour, baking soda, sugar, eggs, milk and chocolate.

B. Do not place commas before the first element of a series or after the last element.

> **Wrong:** My investment adviser recommended that I construct a portfolio of, stocks, bonds, commodities futures, and precious metals.

> **Wrong:** The elephants, tigers, and dancing bears, were the highlights of the circus.

C. Use commas to separate two or more adjectives before a noun; do not use a comma after the last adjective in the series.

> **Wrong:** I can't believe you sat through that long, dull, uninspired, movie three times.

> **Correct:** I can't believe you sat through that long, dull, uninspired movie three times.

D. Use commas to set off parenthetical clauses and phrases. (A parenthetical expression is one that is not necessary to the main idea of the sentence.)

> **Correct:** Gordon, who is a writer by profession, bakes an excellent cheesecake.

The main idea is that Gordon bakes an excellent cheesecake. The intervening clause merely serves to identify Gordon; thus, it should be set off with commas.

**Correct:**    The newspaper that has the most insipid editorials is the *Daily Times*.

**Correct:**    The newspaper, which has the most insipid editorials of any I have read, won numerous awards last week.

In the first of these examples, the clause beginning with *that* defines which paper the author is discussing. In the second example, the main point is that the newspaper won numerous awards, and the intervening clause beginning with *which* identifies the paper.

E. Use commas after introductory participial or prepositional phrases.

**Correct:**    Having watered his petunias every day during the drought, Harold was very disappointed when his garden was destroyed by insects.

**Correct:**    After the banquet, Harold and Martha went dancing.

F. Use commas to separate independent clauses (clauses that could stand alone as complete sentences) connected by coordinate conjunctions such as *and*, *but*, *not*, *yet*, and the like.

**Correct:**    Susan's old car has been belching blue smoke from the tailpipe for two weeks, but it has not broken down yet.

*Note:* Make sure the comma separates two *independent* clauses joined by a conjunction. It is incorrect to use a comma to separate the two parts of a compound verb.

**Wrong:**    Barbara went to the grocery store, and bought two quarts of milk.

### Exercise 12: Commas

Correct the punctuation errors in the following sentences:

1. It takes a friendly energetic person to be a successful sales representative.

2. I was shocked to discover that a large, modern, glass-sheathed, office building had replaced my old school.

3. The country club, a cluster of ivy-covered whitewashed buildings was the site of the president's first speech.

4. Pushing through the panicked crowd the security guards frantically searched for the suspect.

5. Despite careful analysis of the advantages and disadvantages of each proposal Harry found it hard to reach a decision.

## PRINCIPLE 13: USE SEMICOLONS CORRECTLY

When using a semicolon, follow these rules:

A. Use a semicolon *instead of* a coordinate conjunction such as *and*, *or*, or *but* to link two closely related independent clauses.

| | |
|---|---|
| **Wrong:** | Whooping cranes are an endangered species; and they are unlikely to survive if we continue to pollute. |
| **Correct:** | Whooping cranes are an endangered species; there are only fifty whooping cranes in New Jersey today. |
| **Correct:** | Whooping cranes are an endangered species, and they are unlikely to survive if we continue to pollute. |

B. Use a semicolon between independent clauses connected by words like *therefore*, *nevertheless*, and *moreover*.

| | |
|---|---|
| **Correct:** | Farm prices have been falling rapidly for two years; nevertheless, the traditional American farm is not in danger of disappearing. |

### Exercise 13: Semicolons

Correct the punctuation errors in the following sentences:

1. Morgan has five years' experience in karate; but Thompson has even more.

   _____

2. Very few students wanted to take the class in physics, only the professor's kindness kept it from being canceled.

   _____

3. You should always be prepared when you go on a camping trip, however you must avoid carrying unnecessary weight.

   _____

## Principle 14: Use Colons Correctly

When using a colon, follow these rules:

A. In formal writing, the colon is used only as a means of signaling that what follows is a list, definition, explanation, or concise summary of what has gone before. The colon usually follows an independent clause, and it will frequently be accompanied by a reinforcing expression like *the following*, *as follows*, or *namely* or by an explicit demonstrative like *this*.

| | |
|---|---|
| **Correct:** | Your instructions are as follows: read the passage carefully, answer the questions on the last page, and turn over your answer sheet. |
| **Correct:** | This is what I found in the refrigerator: a moldy lime, half a bottle of stale soda, and a jar of peanut butter. |
| **Correct:** | The biggest problem with America today is apathy: the corrosive element that will destroy our democracy. |

B. Be careful not to put a colon between a verb and its direct object.

| | |
|---|---|
| **Wrong:** | I want: a slice of pizza and a small green salad. |
| **Correct:** | This is what I want: a slice of pizza and a small green salad. (The colon serves to announce that a list is forthcoming.) |

| | |
|---|---|
| **Correct:** | I don't want much for lunch: just a slice of pizza and a small green salad. (Here what follows the colon defines what "don't want much" means.) |

C. Context will occasionally make clear that a second independent clause is closely linked to its predecessor, even without an explicit expression like those used above. Here, too, a colon is appropriate, although a period will always be correct also.

| | |
|---|---|
| **Correct:** | We were aghast: the "charming country inn" that had been advertised in such glowing terms proved to be a leaking cabin full of mosquitoes. |
| **Correct:** | We were aghast. The "charming country inn" that had been advertised in such glowing terms proved to be a leaking cabin full of mosquitoes. |

## Exercise 14: Colons

Edit these sentences so they use colons correctly:

1. I am sick and tired of: your whining, your complaining, your nagging, your teasing, and, most of all, your barbed comments.

   _____

2. The chef has created a masterpiece, the pasta is delicate yet firm, the mustard greens are fresh, and the medallions of veal are melting in my mouth.

   _____

3. To write a good essay, you must: practice, get plenty of sleep, and eat a good breakfast.

   _____

## PRINCIPLE 15: USE HYPHENS AND DASHES CORRECTLY

When using a hyphen or a dash, follow these rules:

A. Use the hyphen with the compound numbers twenty-one through ninety-nine and with fractions used as adjectives.

| | |
|---|---|
| **Correct:** | Sixty-five students constituted a majority. |
| **Correct:** | A two-thirds vote was necessary to carry the measure. |
| **Wrong:** | Only two-thirds of the students passed the final exam. |

B. Use the hyphen with the prefixes *ex*, *all*, and *self* and with the suffix *elect*.

| | |
|---|---|
| **Correct:** | The constitution protects against self-incrimination. |
| **Correct:** | The president-elect was invited to chair the meeting. |

C. Use the hyphen with a compound adjective when it comes before the word it modifies but not when it comes after the word it modifies.

| | |
|---|---|
| **Correct:** | The no-holds-barred argument continued into the night. |
| **Correct:** | The argument continued with no holds barred. |

D. Use the hyphen with any prefix used before a proper noun or adjective.

| | |
|---|---|
| **Correct:** | They believed that his activities were un-American. |

E. Use a hyphen to separate component parts of a word to avoid confusion with other words or to avoid the use of a double vowel.

| | |
|---|---|
| **Correct:** | The sculptor was able to re-form the clay after the dog knocked over the bust. |
| **Correct:** | They had to be re-introduced, since it had been so long since they last met. |

F.  Use the dash to indicate an abrupt change of thought. In general, however, formal writing is best when you think out what you want to say in advance and avoid abrupt changes of thought.

> **Correct:**   To get a high score—and who doesn't want to get a high score?—you need to devote yourself to prolonged and concentrated study.

### Exercise 15: Hyphens and Dashes

Edit these sentences so they use hyphens and dashes correctly:

1.  The child was able to count from one to ninety nine.

2.  The adults only movie was banned from commercial TV.

3.  It was the first time she had seen a movie that was for adults-only.

4.  A two thirds majority would be needed to pass the budget reforms.

5.  The house, and it was the most dilapidated house that I had ever seen was a bargain because the land was so valuable.

## PRINCIPLE 16: USE THE APOSTROPHE CORRECTLY

When using an apostrophe, follow these rules:

A.  Use the apostrophe with contracted forms of verbs to indicate that one or more letters have been eliminated in writing. But try to avoid contractions altogether on the GMAT. (See also Principle 11: Avoid Slang and Colloquialisms.)

> **Full Forms:**
>
> *you are*   *it is*   *you have*   *the boy is*
> *Harry has*   *we would*   *was not*
>
> **Contracted:**
>
> *you're*   *it's*   *you've*   *the boy's*
> *Harry's*   *we'd*   *wasn't*

One of the most common errors involving use of the apostrophe is using it in the contraction *you're* or *it's* to indicate the possessive form of *you* or *it*. When you write *you're*, ask yourself whether you mean *you are*. If not, the correct word is *your*. Similarly, are you sure you mean *it is*? If not, use the possessive form *its*. You spell *his* or *hers* without an apostrophe, so you should spell *its* without an apostrophe.

| | |
|---|---|
| **Incorrect:** | You're chest of drawers is ugly. |
| **Incorrect:** | The dog hurt it's paw. |
| **Correct:** | Your chest of drawers is ugly. |
| **Correct:** | The dog hurt its paw. |

B. Use the apostrophe to indicate the possessive form of a noun.

**Not Possessive:**

| | | | |
|---|---|---|---|
| *the boy* | *Harry* | *the children* | *the boys* |

**Possessive Form:**

| | | | |
|---|---|---|---|
| *the boy's* | *Harry's* | *the children's* | *the boys'* |

| | |
|---|---|
| **Correct:** | Ms. Fox's office is on the first floor. (One person possesses the office.) |
| **Correct:** | The Foxes' apartment has a wonderful view. (There are several people named Fox living in the same apartment. First you must form the plural, then add the apostrophe to indicate possession.) |

C. The apostrophe is used to indicate possession only with nouns; in the case of pronouns, there are separate possessives for each person and number.

| | |
|---|---|
| *my, mine* | *our, ours* |
| *your, yours* | *your, yours* |
| *his, his* | *their, theirs* |
| *her, hers* | |
| *its its* | |

The exception is the neutral "one," which forms its possessive by adding an apostrophe and an *s*.

### Exercise 16: Apostrophes

Edit these sentences so they use apostrophes correctly:

1. The presidents limousine had a flat tire.

2. You're tickets for the show will be at the box office.

3. The opportunity to change ones lifestyle does not come often.

4. The desks' surface was immaculate, but it's drawers were messy.

5. The cat on the bed is hers'.

## ANSWERS TO EXERCISES

### Answers to Exercise 1: Wordy Phrases

1. Since John has prepared for this presentation so carefully, we should award him the project.

2. Flights are always at least an hour late on this airline, though its leaders promise that promptness is a high priority for all its employees.

3. Although she is inexperienced in photography, she will probably succeed because she is motivated.

4. Accuracy is important to English teachers and company presidents alike.

5. Humans kill each other because they fear those whom they do not understand.

### Answers to Exercise 2: Redundancy

1. All these problems have combined to create a crisis.

2. A staff that large needs an effective supervisor.

3. He knows how to follow directions.

4. The recent trend of spending on credit has created a poorer middle class.

5. Few people can follow directions.

### Answers to Exercise 3: Excessive Qualification

1. She is a good teacher.

2. Ferrara is a slow worker.

3. You are the best person to decide what you should do for a living.

4. Children should be taught to cooperate at home and in school. (If there's no need to say it, don't!)

5. The travel agent said not to go to Tripoli, since one may be hurt. (Saying *it is possible that one may be hurt* is an example of redundant qualification, since both *possible* and *may* indicate uncertainty.)

## Answers to Exercise 4: Unnecessary Sentences

1. People cannot safely consume water that contains chemical pollutants.

2. No present evidence suggests that Shakespeare's plays were written by others.

3. The United States should send soldiers to areas of conflict.

4. The architect Frank Lloyd Wright was famous for his ability to design buildings that blend into their surroundings.

5. A lot of people find math a difficult subject because it requires very precise thinking skills.

## Answers to Exercise 5: Needless Self-Reference

1. This argument cannot be generalized to most business owners.

2. Food is the best social lubricant.

3. Privacy should not be valued more than social concerns.

4. Most people want to do good work, but many are bored or frustrated with their jobs.

5. The author has a point.

## Answers to Exercise 6: Undesirable Passives

1. Recent allegations of corruption have hurt the politician's standing in the polls.

2. Congress passed the bill in time, but the president did not sign it until the time for action had passed.

3. Those who need advice least usually request it; the truly lost and ignorant do not seek it.

4. The city clerk should take the minutes of the city council meeting.

5. A number of field anthropologists and marriage experts compiled the report.

## Answers to Exercise 7: Weak Openings

1. Businesses ignore the illiteracy problem at their own peril.

2. The government cannot fight a drug war effectively without waging a battle against demand for illicit substances.

3. The candidate has many strong points; intelligence, unfortunately, is not among them.

4. We, as a society, have decided to tolerate homelessness.

5. Americans must like watching television better than conversing.

## Answers to Exercise 8: Needlessly Vague Language

1. When water is heated to 100° C, it turns into steam.

2. The diplomat had to agree to live wherever the government sent him.

3. The principal told John not to return to school until he was ready to behave.

4. The police detective had to ask the lawyer for permission to question the suspect.

5. The last ice age destroyed thousands of animal species.

## Answers to Exercise 9: Clichés

1. Jefferson was a great leader.

2. Trying to find the employee responsible for this embarrassing information leak may be impossible.

3. The military should diversify its defense rather than rely so heavily on nuclear missiles.

4. Older doctors should be required to update their techniques, but many seem resistant to changes in technology.

5. I estimate that 120,000 fans were in the stadium. (Even when a cliché is used in its original context, it sounds old.)

## Answers to Exercise 10: Jargon

1. We expect to use hundreds of paper clips in the next two months.

2. Our schoolchildren's education has been neglected.

3. Foreign diplomats should always talk to local leaders.

4. Recent studies suggest that Vienna sausages are good for you.

5. Government regulatory agencies lied in their press releases about the recent railway accident.

## Answers to Exercise 11: Slang and Colloquialisms

1. Cynthia Larson is an expert.

2. Normal human beings cannot tolerate repeated humiliation.

3. If you want a good cheesecake, you must make a superb crust.

4. International organizations should try to cooperate on global issues like hunger.

5. The environmentalists are not involved in the project for prestige; they truly care about protecting the yellow-throated hornswoggler.

## Answers for Exercise 12: Commas

1. It takes a friendly, energetic person to be a successful sales representative.

2. I was shocked to discover that a large, modern, glass-sheathed office building had replaced my old school.

3. The country club, a cluster of ivy-covered, whitewashed buildings, was the site of the president's first speech.

4. Pushing through the panicked crowd, the security guards frantically searched for the suspect.

5. Despite careful analysis of the advantages and disadvantages of each proposal, Harry found it hard to reach a decision.

## Answers for Exercise 13: Semicolons

1. Morgan has five years' experience in karate; Thompson has even more.

2. Very few students wanted to take the class in physics; only the professor's kindness kept it from being canceled.

3. You should always be prepared when you go on a camping trip; however, you must avoid carrying unnecessary weight.

## Answers to Exercise 14: Colons

1. I am sick and tired of your whining, your complaining, your nagging, your teasing, and, most of all, your barbed comments.

2. The chef has created a masterpiece: the pasta is delicate yet firm, the mustard greens are fresh, and the medallions of veal are melting in my mouth.

3. To write a good essay, you must do the following: practice, get plenty of sleep, and eat a good breakfast.

## Answers to Exercise 15: Hyphens and Dashes

1. The child was able to count from one to ninety-nine.

2. The adults-only movie was banned from commercial TV.

3. It was the first time she had seen a movie that was for adults only.

4. A two-thirds majority would be needed to pass the budget reforms.

5. The house—and it was the most dilapidated house that I had ever seen—was a bargain because the land was so valuable.

## Answers to Exercise 16: Apostrophes

1. The president's limousine had a flat tire.

2. Your tickets for the show will be at the box office.

3. The opportunity to change one's lifestyle does not come often.

4. The desk's surface was immaculate, but its drawers were messy.

5. The cat on the bed is hers.

# APPENDIX 3: COMMON GMAT IDIOMS

*Note*: All of the following have been known to appear on more than one GMAT. Entries with double ellipses (such as between . . . and . . .) indicate that the idiom also sets up a parallelism (between A and B).

### ABLE TO (ABILITY TO)

No one has been *able to* prove that the person who wrote Shakespeare's plays was named Shakespeare.

### AMONG VERSUS BETWEEN

Use *between* when referring to two items or groups, *among* when referring to three or more.

Don't make me choose *between* Tweedledum and Tweedledee.
*Among* all five candidates, he's by far the best qualified.

### AMOUNT VERSUS NUMBER

Use *amount* when referring to an uncountable quantity, like soup or love, and *number* when referring to countable things, like jelly beans or people.

The *amount* of work you put into your studies will affect the *number* of points you will add to your GMAT score.

### AS VERSUS LIKE

Use *like* to compare nouns; use *as* to compare actions—in other words, use *as* when what follows is a clause.

*Like* fine wine, fruitcake tastes better after it has aged.
Dogs don't scratch up furniture, *as* cats often do.

**AS . . . AS**

She actually is *as* naïve *as* she appears.

**ASSOCIATE WITH**

Many people *associate* the smell of vinegar *with* coloring Easter eggs.

**AT LEAST AS . . . AS**

The Eiffel Tower is *at least as* tall *as* the Statue of Liberty.

**ATTRIBUTE TO**

I *attribute* his success *to* having good friends in high places.

**BELIEVE TO BE**

The expert *believes* the painting *to be* a fraud.

**BETWEEN . . . AND . . .**

You must decide *between* wealth *and* fame.

**BOTH VERSUS EACH**

Use *both* when pointing out similarities; use *each* when pointing out differences.
Note that *each* is always singular.

Although *both* cooks enjoy making goulash, *each* has a different take on this
classic dish.

**BOTH . . . AND . . .**

He is *both* an artist *and* a rogue.

**COMPARE TO VERSUS COMPARE WITH**

On the GMAT, *compare with* is the generally preferred form. Use *compare to* to point
out an abstract or figurative likeness and *compare with* to consider likenesses and
differences in general.

Shall I *compare* thee *to* a summer's day?
*Compared with* a summer's day, it's cold outside.

**CONNECTION BETWEEN**

I saw little *connection between* her words and her deeds.

**CONSEQUENCE OF**

One *consequence of* the Supreme Court decision was increased public distrust in the judicial system.

**CONSIDER**

I *consider* you a very good friend.

*Note*: Although *consider to be* is also correct, it will never be correct on the GMAT.

**CONTINUE TO**

Do not *continue to* deny the obvious.

**CONTRAST WITH**

I like to *contrast* my plaid pants *with* a lovely paisley jacket.

**CREDIT WITH**

James Joyce is often *credited with* the invention of the literary form called stream of consciousness.

**DEBATE OVER**

This idiom only applies when *debate* is used as a noun.

They held a lively *debate over* whom to throw off the island.

**DECIDE TO**

She *decided to* go to the party after all.

**DEFINE AS**

My dictionary *defines* a clause *as* group of words containing a subject and a verb.

**DIFFERENT FROM**

John Major's policies were not very *different from* those of Margaret Thatcher.

**DIFFICULT TO**

It's *difficult to* disagree with such a persuasive argument.

**DISPUTE OVER**

This idiom applies only when *dispute* is used as a noun.

The *dispute over* how to read the punchcards was never properly resolved.

**DISTINGUISH BETWEEN . . . AND . . .**

Some color-blind people cannot *distinguish between* red *and* green.

**DISTINGUISH . . . FROM . . .**

Other color-blind people find it difficult to *distinguish* blue *from* purple.

**DOUBLE VERSUS TWICE (TRIPLE VERSUS THREE TIMES, ETC.)**

On the GMAT, *double* (*triple*, *quadruple*, etc.) is only used as a verb; when making a comparison, the preferred form is *twice* (*three times*, etc.).

He promised to *double* the company's profits in less than a year.
I ate *twice* as much as you did.

**EACH (SEE BOTH VERSUS EACH ABOVE.)**

**EACH OTHER VERSUS ONE ANOTHER**

In GMAT English, *each other* is used to refer to two things, and *one another* is used for three or more.

Those two theories contradict *each other*.
Those three theories contradict *one another*.

**EITHER . . . OR . . .**

Today I will *either* look for a job *or* watch the Boston marathon on TV.

**-ER THAN**

Winston Churchill was a bett*er* dancer *than* Neville Chamberlain ever was.

**EXTENT TO WHICH**

You should appreciate the *extent to which* the same idioms repeatedly appear on the GMAT.

**ESTIMATE TO BE**

The oldest cave paintings known to exist are *estimated to be* over 50,000 years old.

**FEWER VERSUS LESS**

Use *fewer* to describe countable things, like jelly beans or people, and *less* to describe an uncountable quantity, like soup or love. (See amount versus number above.)

I ate *fewer* hotdogs and *less* potato salad than I did at last year's picnic.

**FORBID TO**

I was *forbidden to* discuss politics at the dinner table.

**FROM . . . TO . . .**

*From* the redwood forest *to* the Gulf Stream waters, this land was made for you and me.

**JUST AS . . . SO TOO . . .**

*Just as* sand flows through an hourglass, *so too* flow the days of our lives.

**IF VERSUS WHETHER**

If you're ever given a choice on the GMAT, choose *whether*. The actual rule states that whenever you're discussing a choice between alternatives, you should use *whether* (as in *whether or not* to do something) rather than *if*. On the GMAT, *if* is reserved for conditional "if-then" statements.

Let me know *if* I behave inappropriately in front of the royal family. (Translation: I may or may not behave inappropriately, but if I do, then I should be informed).

Tell me *whether* I behaved inappropriately in front of the royal family. (Translation: Either I behaved inappropriately or I didn't; tell me the truth.)

## IN DANGER OF

Conservationists fear that the West Indian manatee is *in danger of* becoming extinct.

## LESS (SEE FEWER VERSUS LESS ABOVE.)

## LIKE VERSUS SUCH AS

If you're ever given a choice on the GMAT, choose *such as*. The GMAT writers prefer *such as* to *like* when what follows are examples; to these writers, *like* means "similar to."

I prefer salty snacks *such as* potato chips to sweet snacks *such as* candy bars.
I've never met anyone *like* him before.

## LIKELY TO

You're *likely to* do well on the GMAT verbal section.

## LINK TO

Exposure to classical music has been *linked to* improved performance on mathematical aptitude tests.

## MODEL AFTER

Louisiana's legal system is *modeled after* the Napoleonic Code.

## MORE THAN

I was *more* prepared this time *than* I was the last time I took the test.

## NATIVE

Use *native to*, meaning "indigenous to," when discussing plants, animals, and the like. Use *a native of* when discussing people and where they were born.

The sugar maple is *native to* Canada.
Leslie Nielsen is *a native of* Canada.

## NEITHER . . . NOR . . .

Note that when a sentence has a *neither . . . nor . . .* subject, whatever follows *nor* determines whether the verb is singular or plural. (The same thing is true of *either . . . or . . .* subjects.)

*Neither* the players *nor* the coach was surprised by the team's victory.

**NOT . . . BUT [RATHER, MERELY] . . .**

It's *not* a bother *but rather* an honor to serve you.

**NOT ONLY . . . BUT ALSO . . .**

I am *not only* charming *but also* modest to a fault.

**NOT SO . . . AS**

It's *not so* bad *as* it seems.

**NOT SO MUCH . . . AS . . .**

The company's recent success is due *not so much* to better management *as* to an improved economy.

**NUMBER (SEE AMOUNT VERSUS NUMBER ABOVE.)**

Also note that on the GMAT *the number of* will always be singular, while *a number of* will always be plural.

> *The number of* stars in our galaxy *is* huge.
> *A number of* guests *are* waiting in the foyer.

**ONE ANOTHER (SEE EACH OTHER VERSUS ONE ANOTHER ABOVE.)**

**OPPOSITION TO**

There has been far less *opposition* in the United States than in Europe *to* the use of genetically modified foods.

**PERCEIVE AS**

I didn't mean for my comments to be *perceived as* criticism.

**PROHIBIT FROM**

People are *prohibited from* entering the park after 10 PM.

**RANGE FROM . . . TO . . .**

Scores on the GMAT *range from* 200 *to* 800.

**REGARD AS**

I *regard* him *as* little more than a common criminal.

**REQUIRE TO**

The laws in many states *require* couples *to* have their blood tested before getting married.

**RESISTANCE TO**

Stress can lower one's *resistance to* cold and flu viruses.

**SAME AS**

I got the *same* score *as* he did.

**SEEM TO**

He *seemed to* be at a loss for words.

**SO . . . AS TO BE . . .**

My new computer game is *so* entertaining *as to be* genuinely addictive.

**SO . . . THAT**

In fact, it's *so* addictive *that* I spend several hours every day playing it.

**SUCH AS (SEE LIKE VERSUS SUCH AS ABOVE.)**

**SUPERIOR TO**

Superman's powers are clearly *superior to* those of Batman.

**TARGET AT**

I sometimes suspect that beer ads are *targeted at* morons.

**THE -ER . . . THE -ER . . .**

*The* bigg*er* they come, *the* hard*er* they fall, or so I have heard.

**TRY TO**

*Try to* write a short story based on your travel experiences.

**TWICE (SEE DOUBLE VERSUS TWICE ABOVE.)**

### USE AS

Lacking cooking implements, we *used* one of the car's hubcaps *as* a makeshift pan.

### VIEW AS

Many *view* the former publishing magnate *as* a con artist extraordinaire.

### WHETHER (SEE IF VERSUS WHETHER ABOVE.)

### WORRY ABOUT

There's no need to *worry about* idioms on the GMAT; just study the ones you don't recognize.

# IDIOMS QUIZ

1.  Richard Gere portrays not only an officer (and also, and as well, but also) a gentleman in this film.

2.  I respect Jerry Hallowell, aka, Ginger Spice, both as an entertainer (and also, and as, but also as) a humanitarian.

3.  I must have either Twinkies™ (or else, or, and) Dingdongs™ for lunch.

4.  You must decide (between, among) the hot and sour soup (or, and) the egg drop soup.

5.  (Between, Among) the three starting pitchers, Martinez is generally (considered, considered to be, considered as) the (more, most) reliable.

6.  There were (less, fewer) immigrants entering the country last year than the previous year.

7.  The (number, amount) of students in my class (has, have) gone up.

8.  I regard the movies of Mamie Van Doren (as, to be, as being) superior (when compared to, over, to) those of Jayne Mansfield.

9.  Poor Zeppo is often perceived (as, to be, as being) the least talented of the Marx Brothers.

10. According to exit polls, a majority of those who voted for the winning candidate viewed him (as, to be, as being) the lesser of two evils.

11. Adam Sandler's movies are not very different (than, from) those of Paulie Shore.

12. It was so quiet (you, that you, as a result you) could hear a pin drop.

13. Barbra Streisand and Neil Diamond (each, both) went to the same high school.

14. Dean Martin and Jerry Lewis (both had their, each had his) own take on why the two split up.

15. Some pundits like to associate the 1960s (with, and) the decline of Western civilization.

16. We held a spirited debate (over, about, concerning) the place of *Married with Children* within the pantheon of classic situational comedies.

17. I can assure you that it was not a dispute (over, about, concerning) trivial issues.

18. Charles was forbidden (to enter, from entering) the Temple of Doom.

19. He was also prohibited (to visit, from visiting) the Garden of Earthly Delights.

20. I hereby define a "baker's dozen" (to be, as, as being) thirteen.

21. Yogi Bear was clearly more intelligent (compared to, as, than) your average bear.

22. Studying grammar is about as pleasant (when compared to, as, than) going to the dentist.

23. I attribute my stunning success (as due to, because of, to) good looks and native intelligence.

24. I attribute my good looks not so much to exquisite grooming (as, but, but rather) to an inner radiance.

25. Most people credit Philo Taylor Farnsworth (as, for, with) having invented the television back in the 1920s while he was still a teenager.

26. Swing dances from the 1940s, (like, such as) the jitterbug and the hucklebuck, have recently become popular again.

27. (Similar to, Like, As with) many female supermodels, Fabio (is also, is) known by his first name alone.

28. I did not try the clam dip, (as, like) my roommate who got sick did.

29. I've finally decided (on going, to go) camping over the holidays, but I still haven't figured out (whether, if) I need to buy a tent.

30. Resistance (against, to) assimilation by the Borg is futile.

# ANSWERS

1. Richard Gere portrays *not only* an officer *but also* a gentleman in this film.

2. I respect Jerry Hallowell, aka, Ginger Spice, both as an entertainer *and as* a humanitarian.

3. I must have either Twinkies™ *or* Dingdongs™ for lunch.

4. You must decide *between* the hot and sour soup *and* the egg drop soup.

5. *Among* the three starting pitchers, Martinez is generally *considered* the *most* reliable.

6. There were *fewer* immigrants entering the country last year than the previous year.

7. The *number* of students in my class *has* gone up.

8. I regard the movies of Mamie Van Doren *as* superior *to* those of Jayne Mansfield.

9. Poor Zeppo is often *perceived as* the least talented of the Marx Brothers.

10. According to exit polls, a majority of those who voted for the winning candidate viewed him *as* the lesser of two evils.

11. Adam Sandler's movies are not very different *from* those of Paulie Shore.

12. It was so quiet *that you* could hear a pin drop.

13. Barbra Streisand and Neil Diamond *both* went to the same high school.

14. Dean Martin and Jerry Lewis *each had his* own take on why the two split up.

15. Some pundits like to associate the 1960s *with* the decline of Western civilization.

16. We held a spirited debate *over* the place of *Married with Children* within the pantheon of classic situational comedies.

17. I can assure you that it was not a dispute *over* trivial issues.

18. Charles was forbidden *to enter* the Temple of Doom.

19. He was also prohibited *from visiting* the Garden of Earthly Delights.

20. I hereby define a "baker's dozen" *as* thirteen.

21. Yogi Bear was clearly more intelligent *than* your average bear.

22. Studying grammar is about as pleasant *as* going to the dentist.

23. I attribute my stunning success *to* good looks and native intelligence.

24. I attribute my good looks not so much to exquisite grooming *as* to an inner radiance.

25. Most people credit Philo Taylor Farnsworth *with* having invented the television back in the 1920s while he was still a teenager.

26. Swing dances from the 1940s, *such as* the jitterbug and the hucklebuck, have recently become popular again.

27. *Like* many female supermodels, Fabio *is* known by his first name alone.

28. I did not try the clam dip, *as* my roommate who got sick did.

29. I've finally decided *to go* camping over the holidays, but I still haven't figured out *whether* I need to buy a tent.

30. Resistance *to* assimilation by the Borg is futile.